RIPLEY'S
Believe It or Not!®

Dare to Discover

RIPLEY
PUBLISHING
a Jim Pattison Company

DARE TO SHARE

Welcome, curious explorer! Did you know that each and every one of us holds something truly extraordinary inside?

Just like the amazing people, places, and animals in this book, you have your own unique traits waiting to be discovered. We dare you to take a moment and think about what makes you unbelievable! Maybe it's your creativity, kindness, or a quirky talent? Whatever it may be, embrace it! Our differences are what makes our world such a fun and exciting place. So, dive into the adventure of self-discovery and uncover the amazing things that make you, well, you!

SHOW US YOUR BELIEVE IT OR NOT!

Do you have a strange-but-true fact, an unbelievable story, a unique talent, or a remarkable discovery? Share it with Ripley's Believe It or Not! for a chance to be featured!

A BELIEVE IT OR NOT! IS SOMETHING VERY HARD TO BELIEVE, BUT TOTALLY TRUE!

SCAN TO SHARE!

BELIEVE IT OR NOT, YOU'RE ONE OF A KIND!

YOU COULD BE IN RIPLEY'S!

Need some inspiration? These amazing people shared their Believe It or Not! with us and ended up in a Ripley's annual book! Could you be next?

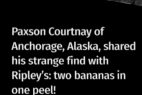

WAVE Asian Bistro & Sushi creates viral sushi items—from sushi pizza to sushi hot dogs and even sushi versions of your favorite pop-culture characters!

Paxson Courtnay of Anchorage, Alaska, shared his strange find with Ripley's: two bananas in one peel!

Balanced atop thin-necked bottles, LadyBEAST seems to effortlessly walk and dance across their narrow, uncorked openings.

THIS COULD BE YOU!

Dear Mr. Ripley

Fan submissions have always been an important and special part of Ripley's Believe It or Not!

At the height of their popularity, Robert Ripley's Believe It or Not! cartoons were read by over 80 million people! They were translated into 17 languages and printed in more than 360 newspapers around the world. Many readers submitted their own unbelievable facts to Ripley, too. In 1929, he received one million letters—that's more than 2,700 messages per day!

CHECK OUT THESE THROWBACK FAN SUBMISSIONS!

BELIEVE IT or NOT

DEAR FRIEND:
THANKS FOR YOUR
SUGGESTION
I HOPE TO USE IT
SOON.
Ripley

SEE PAGE 236!

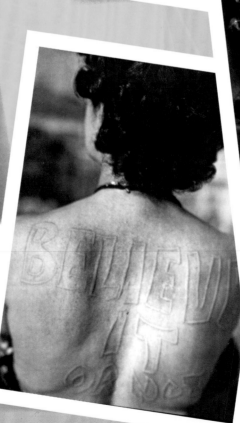

A Believe It or Not! often appears when least expected—like when you're harvesting veggies and find one shaped like a person!

Rosa Barthelme was also called "The Human Slate." Anything lightly etched onto her skin would swell up for several minutes! The condition is known as dermatographia.

Charles Russel of Chicago, Illinois, could hoist his sister with one hand and hold 12 cups of coffee in the other—while balancing on ice skates!

CARTOON CONTEST

In 1932, Ripley launched the first national Believe It or Not! contest. He offered prizes to readers with the best strange-but-true stories. About 2.5 million submissions arrived in just two weeks! The winner was Clinton Blume. He had lost a scrub brush at sea when his Army ship sank off the coast of France. One year later, he found it washed up on a New York beach!

HE WON A PLANE AND FLYING LESSONS!

BELIEVE IT OR NOT—By RIPLEY
(Copyright, 1932)

CLINTON W. BLUME
1400 Ocean Parkway, Brooklyn

LOST A SCRUB BRUSH AT SEA, WHEN ARMY TRANSPORT SANK 500 MILES OFF COAST OF FRANCE, AND IT WAS WASHED ASHORE AT HIS FEET IN BROOKLYN ONE YEAR LATER ! 6-20-32

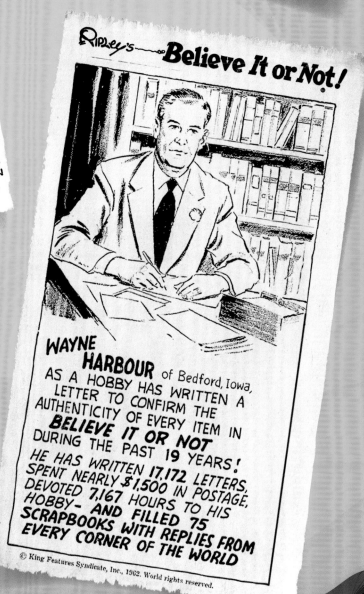

Ripley's Believe It or Not!

WAYNE HARBOUR of Bedford, Iowa, AS A HOBBY HAS WRITTEN A LETTER TO CONFIRM THE AUTHENTICITY OF EVERY ITEM IN **BELIEVE IT OR NOT** DURING THE PAST 19 YEARS! HE HAS WRITTEN 17,172 LETTERS, SPENT NEARLY $1,500 IN POSTAGE, DEVOTED 7,167 HOURS TO HIS HOBBY— AND FILLED 75 SCRAPBOOKS WITH REPLIES FROM EVERY CORNER OF THE WORLD

© King Features Syndicate, Inc., 1962. World rights reserved.

SKEPTIC SNAIL MAIL

Of course, there were haters. Ripley constantly received letters demanding proof of his unbelievable claims. One man, Wayne Harbour, made it his mission to personally prove Ripley wrong! He spent 29 years trying to do so (and even submitted a few cartoon ideas himself). Believe it or not, in nearly three decades of searching, Wayne was never able to debunk a Ripley fact!

Wayne sent 24,241 letters to Robert Ripley!

DISCOVER

There is always something new to discover at Ripley's!
Check out what we've dared to do over the past year!

SEE MORE CRAZY GOLF ON PAGE 162!

DARE TO AMAZE

In Myrtle Beach, South Carolina, Ripley's boasts all-new experiences, from Ripley's Illusion Lab, where optical and interactive illusions come to life, to the quirky Ripley's Crazy Golf.

DARE TO ADVENTURE

Only at Ripley's Aquarium of Myrtle Beach, the all-new Sloth Valley habitat lets you get up close and personal with adorable two-toed sloths!

DARE TO CREATE

Ripley's Art Department has been hard at work on new wax figures, including Kevin Hart and Kim Kardashian.

RIPLEY'S Believe It or Not!®

the World of Ripley's

DARE TO ACHIEVE

Ripley's Aquarium of Canada celebrated 10 years by achieving the Guinness World Records™ title for Longest Underwater Livestream.

DARE TO SAVE

Ripley's Aquarium of the Smokies in Tennessee welcomed the birth of an endangered African penguin! Named Smoky, this cute ball of fluff is part of the Association of Zoos and Aquarium's Species Survival Plan.

CHECK OUT PAGE 71!

DARE TO DANCE

Ripley's recently acquired Prince's iconic purple coat, the pop star's go-to for performances of "Purple Rain."

DARE TO

ACTUAL SIZE!

Pint-Sized Pearl

What's shorter than a popsicle stick and about as long as a dollar bill? If you guessed Pearl the Chihuahua, you'd be correct!

Pearl lives in Orlando, Florida, with her owner, Vanesa Semler. At 3.6 inches (9.1 cm) tall and 5 inches (12.7 cm) long, the tiny dog can be easy to miss. But all eyes were on her in 2023, when she was crowned the shortest living dog in the world! When she was born, Pearl weighed less than 1 ounce (28.3 g). At two years old, the petite pup is just 1.2 pounds (553 g)—this book weighs almost three times that. Pearl may be pocket-sized, but she leaves a big impression!

WE GOT SHRUNK!
Ripley's
Believe It or Not!
ORLANDO, FL

Pearl and her humans at Ripley's Believe It or Not! in Orlando, Florida.

CORN PALACE

You've never seen a place quite so corny as the Corn Palace. Instead of paint, its murals are made of more than 275,000 ears of corn!

Located in Mitchell, South Dakota, the building gets a new set of themed murals almost every year. Artists design the scenes based on the natural colors of local crops. Thankfully, there are at least 12 different shades of corn that can be used, including yellow, white, red, black, and even green! Each ear is nailed to the building one at a time. And the inside has murals, too! The Corn Palace first opened in 1892. Since then, people have come from far and wide to see the a-*maize*-ing artwork that covers the building's walls.

AW, SHUCKS!

WILLIE NELSON!

MILE-HIGH MEALS

Dutch chef Angélique Schmeinck prepares meals hundreds of feet up in the air in a hot-air balloon. Her 10-seater balloon restaurant is called CuliAir, and she uses the flame that powers the balloon to cook food. She makes about 50 balloon trips a year in the Netherlands, with three-course meals served during a 90-minute flight.

SMART MOVE

Rosie, a 10-year-old border collie dog, ran off after being scared by a firework in Loughborough, England, but was later reunited with owners Steve and Julie Harper when she walked into the local police station and sat in the waiting room.

CHEESE PARK

There is a cheese-related theme park in Imsil, South Korea. The 32-acre (13-hectare) park is dedicated to all things cheesy, including a Cheese Playland and centers where visitors can make their own cheese. Cheese was only introduced to South Korea in the late 1950s by a Belgian missionary.

BIZARRE BOXING

In the Russian contact sport of arm boxing, two fighters stand opposite each other while chained at the waist to a podium. Their left hands are taped firmly together, so, as well as being unable to move around much or away from each other, they can only use their right hands to hit their opponent.

ANCIENT SNACK

Fossil evidence from Peruvian caves suggests that popcorn was eaten as far back as 4700 BC—nearly 7,000 years ago.

FLOWER FIND

In 2022, researchers in the Western Himalayas region of India rediscovered a plant species that had not been seen for 188 years. *Brachystelma attenuatum*, a small mountain flower, was first described by two British botanists in 1835 but no specimens had been observed since and so it was thought to have become extinct.

LUCKY TOWN

Mark Cunningham's winning $15.1 million Megabucks lottery ticket in January 2023 was purchased at a store in... Luck, Wisconsin.

DEBT-FREE DEAL

In eighteenth-century Britain and New England, widows sometimes remarried naked or wearing just their underwear or smock in the belief that it would free them from having to pay their late husbands' debts. These events were known as smock weddings.

TRASHY CONTEST

In the Japanese sport of SpoGomi, teams of up to five people wearing heavy duty gloves compete to find who can pick up the most trash from city streets in one hour. At the end, the teams' trash is weighed and checked, and in the event of a tie, the winner is determined by the quality of the collected waste. Cigarette butts earn high points.

BRAISE THE ROOF

Even the biggest hot dog craving can be cured at Wienerlicious! On the roof of this diner in Mackinaw City, Michigan, is a 63-foot-long (19.2-m) frank topped with ketchup, mustard, and more. Made of spray foam, the giant wiener was designed by artist Ron Berman. The diner's owners hired Ron after seeing one of his other works—a 30-foot-tall (9.1-m) bear who just might take a bite of the huge hot dog!

COLOSSAL CABINET

Need to organize some papers? In Burlington, Vermont, there is a filing cabinet that stands more than 40 feet (12.2 m) tall. That's as high as a four-story building! The tower is a sculpture by artist Bren Alvarez. She was inspired by the paperwork and long processes that delayed the building of a new road in the city. She welded 11 metal cabinets together to create the piece, with a total of 38 drawers—the same number of years the road had been in planning at the time!

40 FEET (12.2 M) TALL

WELLIE TOSS

Wellie Wanging takes kicking your shoes off seriously! The game, which began in Yorkshire, England, is named after the Wellington boot. Whoever can throw their boot the farthest wins! To play, you can stand or get a running start before throwing with one or two hands. Some players like to throw their boot between their legs or even facing backward! People of all ages compete in Wellie Wanging championships every year. Better start practicing!

IT'S ALL A-BOOT HOW FAR YOU CAN TOSS!

EXPERIENCED PLAYER

On April 25, 2022, 79-year-old defender David Mudge played a full 90 minutes for his local soccer team, Kissing Point, in New South Wales, Australia.

MARATHON MIRACLE

Russell Winwood, from Brisbane, Australia, runs full 26.2-mile (42-km) marathons despite only having 30 percent lung capacity due to an incurable medical condition. He runs with a 7-pound (3.2-kg) oxygen tank on his back.

CAKE DRESS

Swiss baker Natasha Coline Kim Fah Lee Fokas created an enormous wearable cake in the form of a wedding dress. The layered cake dress, which weighed 289 pounds (131 kg), could be worn and eaten at the same time.

EXCESS EATING

Every day for 40 days, Alexander Tominsky, from Philadelphia, Pennsylvania, ate an entire rotisserie chicken. At the end of the challenge, he vowed he would never eat another one.

BLIND BOARDER

Skateboarder Daniel Mancina, who is blind, performed a record-breaking 50-50 grind on a rail for a distance of 22.5 feet (6.9 m).

SAME NAMES

Imagine meeting 177 people with the same name as you! On October 29, 2022, 178 people—aged 3 to 80—named Hirokazu Tanaka assembled in Tokyo, Japan. One man traveled all the way from Vietnam—about 2,300 miles (3,701 km) away.

■ GOING TOE-TO-TOE! ■

Ben Woodroffe of Wetton, Derbyshire, was just 14 when he discovered the unlikely sport of toe wrestling, which was founded in his hometown. From then on, he had a big dream: to become the champion. Ben overcame lots of challenges. He faced broken toes, blisters, long matches, and even had both toenails surgically removed (giving him a professional advantage). At age 34, he finally knocked the 17-time champion into retirement and made his childhood dream come true. It's a funny sport, but for Ben, it was a big, proud moment for him and his hometown!

TOE WRESTLING CHAMPION!

CHECKMATE OR KNOCKOUT?

Chess boxing is the best of both worlds: the strategy of chess and the strength of boxing!

In chess boxing, players alternate between rounds of chess and boxing, starting with four minutes of chess, followed by three minutes in the ring. Players need to be smart and strong to play this unique combo sport. They can win by getting a checkmate in chess or knocking out their opponent in boxing. The sport originated in 2003 and has quickly gained popularity around the world, namely in India. However, some believe the sport can be traced back to 1970s London, when two brothers made headlines for playing chess after a boxing match at their gym.

MAKE YOUR MOVE!

Rainbow

There is a colorful creature for every shade of the rainbow—red, orange, yellow, green, blue, indigo, and even violet! From insects to mammals, birds, and more, this list will take you on a rainbow-tinted trip through the animal kingdom!

RED

Found across North America, the red velvet ant has soft hair that is bright orange-red. Even though it's called an ant, it's actually a kind of wasp! It is an easy mistake to make, as the females have ant-like bodies and no wings. They also have a very painful sting, giving the wasp another common name: cow killer ant. So be careful if you spot one in the wild!

ORANGE

The painted bat is named for its bright orange fur that looks like the work of an artist's brush. Found in Southeast Asia, the painted bat is small and hard to spot. Its body is only about 2 inches (5 cm) long! They hunt at night and fly low to the ground. Some people think the orange color helps them blend in with dried leaves on the forest floor!

YELLOW

It's clear to see how the banana slug got its name! It lives in damp forests on North America's west coast. It can grow up to 10 inches (25.4 cm) long but has a top speed of just 6.5 inches (16.5 cm) per minute, making it one of the slowest animals on Earth! Since it can't outrun predators, the slug fights back by filling the mouths of hungry animals with tons of gooey, numbing slime!

GREEN

The common baron caterpillar can make itself almost invisible! It lives on mango leaves in India and nearby countries. Most of its body is bright green, including the fuzzy spines it uses to feel around. It also has a light green or yellow stripe down its back. When the caterpillar lines the stripe up with the center of a mango leaf, it practically disappears!

LOOK! HERE I AM!

BLUE

The cobalt blue tarantula is native to Southeast Asia, but its shiny color makes it a popular pet choice around the world (despite its painful bite). It grows to around 5 inches (12.7 cm) long from toe to toe and lives in holes it digs in the ground. It builds large webs to catch prey such as bugs, lizards, and even small mammals. Scientists think the spider's blue color might be for attracting mates!

INDIGO

During mating season, the male indigo bunting of the Americas is covered in feathers that seem to shimmer in shades of blue and purple. But they aren't really those colors! In bright light, microscopic shapes in the feathers bend and reflect blue light. But in dim light, the feathers show their true colors: brown and black.

VIOLET

The Spanish shawl is a neon-colored sea slug found in the Pacific Ocean. Its main body is bright violet-purple and can grow almost 3 inches (7.6 cm) long. The orange "shawl" on its back is actually a row of organs called cerata. They are a defense against hungry predators and contain stinging cells that the sea slug absorbs from its prey!

Splash ZONE

This swimming pool is so big that you can sail a boat in it!

At 3,324 feet (1,013 m) long, this man-made body of water is longer than nine football fields lined up end to end! The giant pool is part of the San Alfonso Del Mar resort in Algarrobo, Chile. It holds a mind-boggling 66 million gallons (250 million liters) of filtered seawater. Where does the resort get all of that water? From right next door, straight out of the Pacific Ocean!

FLASHY FINS

This fish looks like a floating orange outline! It is the juvenile, or young, stage of a longfin batfish. It lives in the tropical waters of the Indo-West Pacific. As it grows up, the fish turns gray and its fins change shape. But why look different in the first place? It may be a way to trick predators while the fish is too small to defend itself. The orange and black colors make the batfish look a lot like a toxic flatworm—not exactly a tasty meal!

A TOXIC FLATWORM!

Catalog No. 166373

White Squirrel

In the town of Marionville, Missouri, there are hundreds of white squirrels! Some are truly albino, with pink eyes, but others, like the one shown here, simply lack natural color pigments in their fur.

I'M STUCK ON YOU!

Catalog No. 21897

Tiger and Turtle

Looks like this tiger bit off more than it could chew! Tigers are known to play in the water, and they will eat just about anything they can get their paws on. This skull belonged to a tiger that drowned after getting its teeth stuck inside of turtle shell.

Catalog No. 16709

Rare White Moose

This one-in-100,000 white moose was found in Ontario, Canada, in 1985! Although originally thought to be albino, the moose's striking white color is due to an even rarer recessive gene. White animals like this moose are considered sacred by many Indigenous people of North America, such as the Mi'kmaq.

TRIPLE TROUBLE!

ONE IN 100,000!

Catalog No. 175006

Locked Antlers

Three's a crowd! These three fallow deer from a hunting ranch somehow became locked together by their antlers. A deer's antlers' main purpose is to indicate health and age to other deer during their breeding season. But when tensions run high, collisions can happen!

FOOD FOR Thought

SHRIMP!

Chuckie from The Rugrats

New Yorker Harley Langberg makes art that is good enough to eat—literally!

Harley is a dad, husband, and businessman who loves both art and food. In 2013, he saw pictures of food art made by artists Bill and Claire Wurtzel and decided to try it himself. Since then, Harley has created more than 100 pieces! He has found many creative ways to include color and texture in his work. For example, he once used dried anchovies to achieve a shiny silver color! Hungry to know more, Ripley's reached out to Harley and asked him a few questions.

RICE NOODLES!

" Just have fun with it and be proud of what you create.

EDIBLE LIVING ROOM!

SPAGHETTI!

Winifred Sanderson from *Hocus Pocus*

TORTILLA!

Jim Carrey's The Mask

MUSHROOMS!

WAFFLE!

Ed Sheeran

Q: What are some unique challenges you face with your art?

A: Some ingredients are not the easiest to work with, and I learned early on which ones to avoid and which ones to focus on for my pieces. For example, sauces, condiments, and spices are very tricky since they don't hold shape well and are very sensitive to any touch.

Q: What is your favorite piece and why?

A: My portrait of Ed Sheeran. Portraits are always tricky for me because it's a challenge to make someone recognizable just using food. But with this Ed Sheeran piece I felt I nailed it, and everyone recognized who he was immediately. It was definitely my best portrait I have ever created. Ed also happens to be my favorite singer. I also especially loved this piece since I felt I was very creative in the ingredient choices, like Belgian waffles for his shirt.

Q: How long do your artworks take?

A: My pieces usually take between one and two hours to complete.

Q: What has making art taught you that you want to share with our readers?

A: I have learned that art requires patience and time. Success and artistic prowess don't happen overnight. For me, it took several years to get to the level of where I am at now. I look back at my early food art and I think, "Wow, that's what I created? Not good at all!" But it was good at the time, and I had to start somewhere. I would also tell people to not be too hard on themselves. Art should be something fun and relaxing, not something to make you stressed out. Don't get too caught up in making the most perfect piece—just have fun with it and be proud of what you create, because to be able to create anything with your hands is very rewarding and an accomplishment in itself.

BIG Dill

Pickle lovers flock to the city of Pittsburgh, Pennsylvania, every summer to attend Picklesburgh—a festival devoted to the crunchy, tangy food!

A highlight of the festival is the Pickle Juice Drinking contest. The goal is to be the fastest to drink 1 quart (0.95 liters) of pickle juice. The winner is named Mayor of Picklesburgh. In 2022, Jalen Franko of Wisconsin won with a time of just 4.5 seconds! The rest of the festival is packed with pickles used in unexpected ways. Attendees get to enjoy foods such as pickle pizza, fried pickles, pickle grilled cheese, pickle popcorn, pickle eggrolls, and more. There are even desserts! Pickle-flavored cotton candy, ice cream, and fudge are just a few sweet ways to end a day at Picklesburgh.

REPTILE RAWR-MEN

A noodle shop in Taiwan serves a dish topped with a crocodile claw! Known as Godzilla Ramen, the meal looks like the famous Japanese monster is crawling out of the bowl. The special soup is on the menu at Witch Cat Kwai in Douliu City. The restaurant serves only two bowls per day, and they cost around $50 USD each! That is because the crocodile legs are hard to obtain and prepare properly. To cook the claw, the chefs clean it, rub it with spices, and then simmer it in the special broth for two hours. Those who have tried Godzilla Ramen say it tastes like "springy, soft" chicken!

ICE DRINKING COMPETITION

PICKLE FUDGE!

PICKLE MANIA!

PICKLE PIZZA!

SAUSAGE TREE

There's a tree in Africa that grows fruit shaped like giant sausages! You won't be surprised to find out this plant is known as a sausage tree. Anyone walking below its branches should watch their head. The sausage tree's fruit can grow up to 3 feet (0.9 m) long and weigh up to 30 pounds (13.6 kg)— that's about the size of an adult corgi! Its size is not the only thing that makes it a hazard. The fruit can also be poisonous to humans. However, if prepared correctly, it can be very nutritious. Despite its funny name and odd fruit, the sausage tree is an amazingly helpful and important part of African culture.

AtypicalTEMPLE

Thailand's dazzling Wat Rong Khun hides a surprise: paintings and sculptures of pop culture icons such as the Hulk, Freddy Kruger, and even Hello Kitty!

Also known as the White Temple, it is the work of artist Chalermchai Kositpipat. He started in 1997, and he is still adding to it! Its bright white exterior is lined with shiny mirrors. A bridge leads you over a sea of arms to the main building. Inside is a mural of a war between good and evil. The painting includes heroes and villains from *Kung Fu Panda*, *The Matrix*, and many other popular stories. The mix of classic styles and modern media makes for a temple unlike any other.

BATMAN

Pop culture icons are found all over the inside and outside of the temple.

THE PREDATOR

KUNG FU PANDA

RUNNING BLIND

Imagine closing your eyes and then sprinting as fast as you can. Do you think you could stay on the right path or know when you've crossed the finish line if you couldn't see? Probably not! However, that is the reality for some visually impaired runners. But that doesn't mean they can't race. One way these athletes overcome such obstacles is by teaming up with sighted guides. A short tether connects a runner to their guide, which helps them stay on track. A guide can also tell a runner how far they are into a race, what place they are in, and other useful information. Successful pairs, such as those who race in the Paralympic Games, run in perfect sync with each other!

STUMPING THE STREETS

At 74 years old, French carpenter Michel Robillard made a car out of wood and it actually works! Putting in more than 5,000 hours over five years of work, Michel reproduced a popular French classic, the Citroën 2CV. It can travel up to 50 mph (80 kmph) and was sold for €210,000 (around $225,000 USD). Using timber from fruit and nut trees, this was the very first time a functioning wooden car came up for auction—driving up the price!

WOOD YOU LOOK AT THAT!

ICY BLUES

The ice caves of Alaska's Mendenhall Glacier are dangerously beautiful!

They form when the glacier melts and moves, creating cool paths of bright blue ice. The stunning color is due to years of heavy snow pushing air out of the ice. Without air, ice only reflects blue light. But don't let the beauty distract you—exploring ice caves is risky! They change as it gets colder or warmer and can collapse without warning. This danger is being seen more often as climate change causes the glacier to melt faster than it can grow.

CASTLE *Ghosts*

Eerie ghost statues can be found all around the Vezio Castle in Italy!

Every year, people visiting the castle get to help make these ghosts. They put plaster on themselves to make the shapes of the spooky figures! The ghosts stay outside all winter until the next season. Legend has it, the spirit of Queen Theodelinda walks the castle halls. The plastered ghosts are made in her honor.

WHO GHOST THERE?

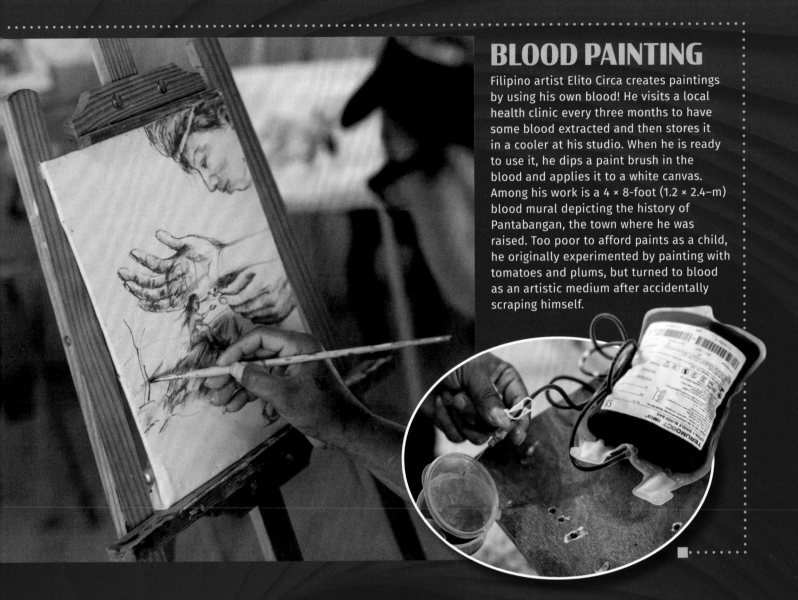

BLOOD PAINTING

Filipino artist Elito Circa creates paintings by using his own blood! He visits a local health clinic every three months to have some blood extracted and then stores it in a cooler at his studio. When he is ready to use it, he dips a paint brush in the blood and applies it to a white canvas. Among his work is a 4 × 8-foot (1.2 × 2.4–m) blood mural depicting the history of Pantabangan, the town where he was raised. Too poor to afford paints as a child, he originally experimented by painting with tomatoes and plums, but turned to blood as an artistic medium after accidentally scraping himself.

NO DUELS

All lawyers and elected officials in Kentucky must swear an oath to say they have never fought a duel with deadly weapons.

TROPHY FOR THE TIRED

To win a lying down championship in 2023, contestants Lidija Marković and Filip Knežević stayed stretched out for 50 days! The annual contest takes place in the village of Brezna, Montenegro. Participants can entertain themselves but are only allowed to stand once every eight hours to go to the bathroom.

MASSIVE MOSAIC

The 410-foot-long (125-m) Selarón Staircase, which links two streets in Rio de Janeiro, Brazil, features more than 2,000 colorful mosaic tiles. The old crumbling staircase was renovated by Chilean artist Jorge Selarón who added tiles in blue, green, and yellow—the colors of the Brazilian flag.

BUTT BUYS

Imagine being able to buy more than 400 poop-themed products! Well, it's possible—at the Unco Shop in Yokohama, Japan, Akihiko Nobata sells poopy T-shirts, sneakers, jewelry, and much more.

EMPEROR'S HEART

In 2022, as part of the 200th anniversary of Brazil's independence, the 188-year-old embalmed heart of its first emperor, Dom Pedro I, was flown in from Portugal to go on public display in Brasilia. It was Pedro, son of the King of Portugal, who declared Brazilian independence from Portugal in 1822. He died in 1834 at age 35, and his heart has been preserved in formaldehyde in a flask in Porto ever since.

BOOK BONANZA

The village of Montolieu in southwest France has more than 800 residents and just over 15 bookshops—about one for every 52 people. It is also home to several museums about books.

EVERLASTING GERMS

If you sneeze or cough whilst climbing Mount Everest, the microbes are preserved in the ice on the mountain for decades.

MALL MAKEOVER

A group of artists led by Michael Townsend lived in Rhode Island's Providence Place Mall for four years before finally being discovered by security guards. They used an empty room beneath the mall that wasn't open to the public and built a cinderblock wall and a utility door to stay hidden. They furnished the room, installed a TV and PlayStation 2, and used the mall's bathrooms for running water.

SINGLE SPECIMEN

Only one 0.01-ounce (0.3-g) specimen of the mineral kyawthuite exists in the world. The transparent, deep orange gem was discovered in the bed of a stream in Myanmar and is currently kept in the Natural History Museum of Los Angeles County.

Catalog No. 174089

Bloodletting Kit

Bloodletting was once a common medical procedure. It involved cutting a patient on purpose to make them bleed, hoping any "impurities" would leave the body. This antique bloodletting kit includes a scarificator, which made multiple cuts at once. Also inside are glass cups and a small lamp. The lamp would heat up the cups, which would be placed over cuts to help draw the "bad blood" out.

SCARIFICATOR

GLASS CUP

LAMP

Catalog No. 18515

Papier-Mâché Model

For a long time, medical students did not have many great options for studying the human body. Real corpses decayed quickly, and wax models began to melt if handled for too long. Papier-mâché models like this open chest were introduced in the 1800s and helped solve those problems! Can you spot the heart, lungs, ribs, and muscles?

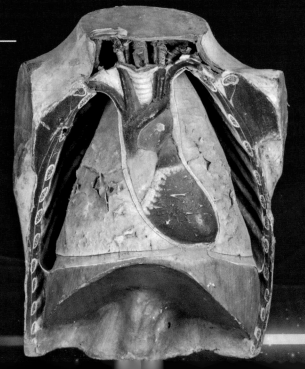

Catalog No. 175795

Iron Lung

The iron lung was developed in 1927 and is best known for helping patients paralyzed by polio. The machine creates an airtight chamber with a patient's head outside, sealed by a collar around the neck. An electric motor forces air in and out of the device. The changes in pressure move the patient's lungs to mimic breathing when their bodies are unable to do so.

ELEPHANT PROSTHETIC

Chhouk is an elephant with a rubber foot! After losing his foot to a snare trap, the Wildlife Alliance in Cambodia gave him a home. The prosthetic came from Paradise Wildlife Park in the UK. It helps Chhouk walk, run, and swim without any trouble. The recycled rubber foot had to be replaced every six months as Chhouk grew up. Each new foot cost almost $1,500 per year, but it has allowed Chhouk to live a comfortable and happy life!

IRON HAND

Scientists discovered a skeleton with an iron hand that was 400 to 600 years old! Found near a church in Bavaria, Germany, the iron hand is an early prosthetic. The person it belonged to was likely a man 30 to 50 years old, living around the years 1450 to 1620. The skeleton also has some missing fingers and signs that the person lost them or needed help. Scientists believe this happened because of battles that took place in the area. People were either injured or had body parts replaced with iron!

X-RAY OF ANCIENT PROSTHETIC!

BIONIC WOMAN

A Swedish woman named Karin is the first person to receive a bionic prosthetic that is fused with the user's bone—and can be controlled with the mind!

Karin lost her arm in a farming accident and struggled with pain and mobility. Made by engineers and doctors from Sweden, Australia, and Italy, her new limb has given her comfort and mobility again. A revolutionary technology, it combines fusing surgery, limb loss, and AI all in one. Karin can now perform 80 percent of what she used to do, like turning a doorknob or cooking a meal. Since the prosthetic is connected to her bones and nerves, she can even feel sensations in the artificial arm!

PUSHING THE LIMITS OF POSSIBILITY!

AI for an EYE

This camera uses words and AI technology to "take" pictures!

The Paragraphica camera was made by Danish designer Bjørn Karmann. To create an image, it first gathers data like the address, weather, and time. It then writes a paragraph based on that information. Finally, it uses artificial intelligence (AI) to turn the text into a picture! The camera's "photos" are not of real places. However, they often have a lot in common with where the picture was made!

The camera's design is based on the star-nosed mole, which is nearly blind but can still "see" using its powerful nose!

A midday photo taken at Cliffordstraat, Amsterdam The weather is partly cloudy and 18 degrees. The date is Wednesday, 24 May, 2023. Near by there is parking and yoga studio.

TEXT TO PICTURE

REAL LOCATION!

AI CREATION!

FACT or FAKE?

What looks like the work of Dr. Strange is actually a rare mutation called fasciation! This artistic twist of nature causes multiple parts of a plant to grow on a single stem.

With the right lighting and crystal-clear waters, boats can look as though they defy gravity and float in the air!

Did photographer Jagdeep Rajput spot a real Pegasus? Not quite! But his photo of a bull being chased by a crane earned him a nod in the 2022 Comedy Wildlife Photography Awards.

WHERE DOES THE WATER COME FROM?

V.I.P. TICKET

Look out below! Planes at the Leipzig/Halle Airport in Germany can take a runway over the famous Autobahn highway as cars cruise by underneath.

How can water be pouring out of this faucet? We won't give away the secret, but you can see it for yourself at several Ripley's Believe It or Not! locations.

HOW DID YOU DO? ⟶ As strange as they seem, all of these photos and facts are totally real!

the stroller-coaster

A ROLLER COASTER WALK IN THE SKY!

While Pohang's Space Walk may look like a roller coaster full of twists, turns, and even loops, this South Korean sculpture is meant to be experienced on foot!

Visitors can take a stroll along the 317-ton steel track to take in the views of Hwanho Park. The Space Walk has 717 total steps and climbs to the height of an eight-story building! From there, the views of Youngil Bay and Youngildae Beach are spectacular! Worried about navigating that upside-down section? Don't be! It's not meant to be walked on and is off-limits.

NO WALKING SECTION!

ECO ART

French contemporary artist Saype's mediums of choice? Grass and eco-responsible paint that he invented himself! He paints incredibly realistic pieces using the environment as his canvas. His paint is made up of water, chalk, coal, and milk protein. It's completely biodegradable, allowing his art to disappear in as little as a month.

STRIKE AT SPEED

In 2019, NASCAR series driver Aric Almirola and Australian pro bowler Jason Belmonte teamed up to bowl a 140-mph (225-kmph) strike from a moving race car at Charlotte Motor Speedway in North Carolina. Almirola drove the car at high speed while Belmonte bowled the ball out of the passenger-side window.

COASTAL CYCLE

Setting off in September 2022, 19-year-old Avery Seuter rode a unicycle all the way down the east coast of the U.S. from Maine to Key West, Florida. His 15-state journey covered 2,400 miles (3,840 km) and took him over four months. His maximum speed on the unicycle was 9 mph (14 kmph).

HOT SHOT

Denmark's Lars Andersen can shoot seven consecutive arrows through a tiny keyhole measuring less than 0.4 inches (10 mm) in diameter. He can also shoot arrows with great accuracy while hanging upside down.

CROSSING CANADA

Ultramarathoner Dave Proctor, of Okotoks, Alberta, ran across Canada in 67.5 days from St. John's, Newfoundland and Labrador, to Victoria, British Columbia—a distance of 4,448 miles (7,158 km). He averaged 66 miles (106 km) a day and wore through 12 pairs of shoes.

REVIVED CAREER

Ray Ruschel revived his high school dream of playing football—30 years after graduating. When the 49-year-old enrolled in a business management course at the North Dakota State College of Science, he discovered that he was eligible to try out for the college football team. After making the team, he played as a defensive lineman for the Wildcats.

LEAP OF LEGENDS

You may know about Holi, the Hindu festival of colors, but what about Holika Dahan? Holika Dahan is celebrated the day before Holi. It is not for the faint of heart! In a ritual representing the burning of a demon, worshipers jump in and out of a 20-foot-tall (6.1-m) fire. A leap for joy, this dangerous stunt symbolizes the victory of good over evil.

COMING IN HOT!

Sand Song

Tourists gather in the hundreds to ride camels on China's Mingsha Mountains, a range of massive sand dunes that sing!

Once used for trade and farming, the camels now take travelers on a special journey. The Mingsha Mountains are on the ancient Silk Road trading route. When the wind blows, these huge sand dunes create amazing sounds—from low hums to loud roars. No one is completely sure what causes the "singing," but there have been many theories. When famous explorer Marco Polo heard the sound in the late 1200s, he thought it was evil spirits!

I'M STUFFED!

BIG BELLY

A honeypot ant eats so much nectar that its abdomen swells to the size of a grape! Gorging on that much food may sound greedy, but it's all for the good of the colony. When food is scarce, these bloated workers regurgitate the nectar so their fellow ants have something to eat!

ELEPHANT TEST

When New York's Brooklyn Bridge opened in 1883, people believed it would collapse. To prove its safety, circus owner P. T. Barnum led 21 elephants across the bridge on May 17, 1884.

COPIOUS CONCRETE

There is enough concrete in the Hoover Dam to build a two-lane highway all the way from San Francisco to New York City—a distance of nearly 3,000 miles (4,800 km). The dam contains nearly 116 million cubic feet (3.3 million cubic m) of concrete.

SEVEN SKIS

At just eight years old, Maddock Lipp, from Colorado, had already gone skiing on all seven continents. He skied on the seventh continent with his family—on Mount Hoegh in Antarctica—in December 2022.

SAHARA NO-SANDS

Only a quarter of Africa's vast Sahara Desert is sandy. Most of it is covered in gravel and rock.

ROUNDABOUT RESIDENCE

For over 40 years, Clwyd Howatson and his family have lived in the middle of a traffic roundabout in Denbighshire, Wales. David John and Eirian Howatson moved into the bungalow in 1960, nearly 20 years before the roundabout was proposed, and refused to move once it was constructed. The family home is surrounded by traffic on all sides.

BUDDHIST BELLS

At midnight on New Year's Eve, Buddhist temples all over Japan ring their bells 108 times. It is part of a ritual called Joya-no-Kane and represents the cleansing of 108 worldly desires which a person is thought to experience throughout their life. When the bell is struck for the 108th time, it is believed to remove all worries and problems from the past year.

PILES OF PIPES

The Grand Organ in the Royal Albert Hall in London, England, is 70 feet (21 m) tall by 65 feet (20 m) wide, weighs 165 tons, and contains 9,999 pipes. If laid end to end, the pipes would stretch for about 9 miles (14.4 km).

DEAD DRONES

Scientists in Socorro, New Mexico, have converted dead birds that have been preserved through taxidermy into bird drones. Because they look like real live birds, the flying drones can join flocks of birds in the air to help study flight patterns.

Henry Cabelus of Long Beach, California, takes the springy sport of extreme pogo to incredible heights!

Using his pumped up pogo stick, Henry can hop higher than 11 feet (3.4 m) into the air. And he doesn't just bounce—he flips, grinds, twists, and kicks! Extreme pogo is a relatively new sport. It's like a mix of skateboarding, BMX, and parkour. The tricks are thrilling, creative, and risky. They are performed at jaw-dropping speeds and heights—and a pogo stick has just the one point to land on! The best pogo athletes compete at Pogopalooza, where Henry has won more than 15 medals. Athletes like Henry push the boundaries of what is possible, turning what was once considered just a toy into a genuine action sport!

POGO PRODIGY

FLIP, GRIND, TWIST, KICK!

GIANT HAIRBALL!

HAIR-RAISER

Divina Burnell of Australia has saved her hair for 23 years, resulting in a giant hairball! The ball is completely made up of hairs that have fallen off her head during showers. She started collecting them so they would stop clogging the drain. More than two decades (and hundreds of showers) later, the hairball is now three times the size of her head! Divina is proud of her collection and shows it off whenever she gets the chance.

SUPERHERO STASH

Miguel Andrés Javier from Peru has a collection of more than 1,500 pieces of memorabilia related to Marvel superhero Iron Man. He started his collection in 2007, a year before the release of the first film.

BODY ART

Designer Amanda Booth from Toronto, Canada, makes items of "body" jewelry—including necklaces, bracelets, and earrings—from human hair, breast milk, umbilical cords, placenta, and human ashes.

SEED SPREADING

Canadian Antoine Moses planted 23,060 trees in 24 hours near High Level, Alberta, at an average of one tree every 3.75 seconds. He has planted more than 1.3 million trees across Canada since 2015.

CHOPPER DROP

Former Australian rules football player Brendan Fevola caught an American football that was dropped from a helicopter hovering 728 feet (222 m) above the ground over Melbourne in Victoria, Australia.

ARMY ART

Canadian artist Dominique Blain's anti-war piece, *Missa*, consists of 100 pairs of army boots hung from a square metal grid on nylon strings. One boot of each pair is raised slightly off the floor to represent a marching army.

MANHATTANHENGE

Four days out of the year, the setting sun lines up perfectly with the streets of New York City to create "Manhattanhenge." The phenomenon was named after Stonehenge in England. There, the sun aligns with the prehistoric monument when it rises on the summer solstice. Manhattanhenge occurs on different dates each year, but usually happens in May and July. On those days, both sides of the street are lit up with sunshine for a few rare moments!

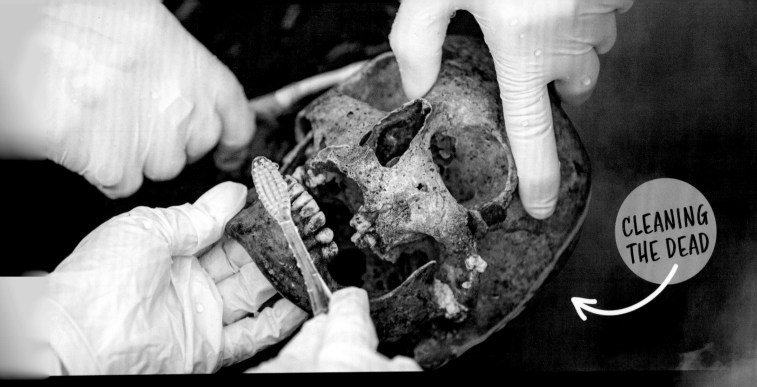

DIGNITY AFTER DEATH

During the Lang Pa Cha ritual to honor the dead, bones are dug up, covered in gold, and then burned in a huge pile.

Practiced in Thailand, the rare ceremony takes place when a cemetery runs out of room. It is a mix of customs from Buddhism and Chinese folk religion. Volunteers dig up the bones of people who had no one to care for them and were buried without a name. The remains are carefully washed, and the skulls are dabbed with gold leaf. The bones are cremated at the end. The ritual is said to bring good luck to the volunteers who help give those unclaimed people a dignified funeral.

MONARCH MATES
Adele Hankey, from North Dakota, was born on April 21, 1926—the same day as Queen Elizabeth II. The two women later became pen pals for 70 years without ever meeting in person. When Elizabeth became Queen in 1952, Adele wrote her a letter and Elizabeth responded by sending a birthday card. From then on, they exchanged handwritten birthday cards and sometimes photos every year. Hankey died in September 2022, less than a month after the death of Elizabeth.

BIG CHEESE
When a New York dairy farmer sent U.S. President Andrew Jackson a 1,400-pound (636-kg) wheel of cheese, it was left in the entrance hall of the White House to age for two years. In 1837, Jackson invited the public to come and eat it, and the entire wheel was devoured in two hours—although the smell lingered in the hall for much longer.

BONE BAR
The HR Giger Bar in Gruyères, Switzerland, is decorated throughout with a skeleton bone design that covers its ceilings, floors, walls, chairs, and even flower vases. The horror movie–inspired bar was designed by Hans Rudi Giger, who worked on the *Alien* movies.

MONSTER PIZZA
YouTuber Airrack and restaurant chain Pizza Hut cooked a pizza so big it was cut into 68,000 slices. The giant pizza was made on the floor of the Los Angeles Convention Center and was then cooked with heat lamps. It covered an area of 13,957.77 square feet (1,296.72 sq m) and was made from 13,653 pounds (6,193 kg) of dough, 4,948 pounds (2,244 kg) of tomato sauce, over 8,800 pounds (3,992 kg) of cheese, and 630,496 pepperoni pieces.

BIG BELLIES
Men among the Bodi tribe of southern Ethiopia fatten themselves up for six months so that they can win an annual festival for the person with the biggest stomach. To prepare for the Ka'el festival, the men feast on a fattening diet of cow's milk, cow's blood, and honey. To obtain the blood, they puncture the cow's vein with a spear, collect the blood in a pot, and then seal the wound with clay so that the animal quickly recovers. Big bellies are considered attractive among the Bodi, and the winner earns the respect of the whole tribe for life.

Catalog No. 15043

Day of the Dead Statue

Dia de los Muertos, or Day of the Dead, is a 3,000-year-old celebration! This statue of St. Francis is colorfully painted with a traditional smiling skeleton face. It was likely placed on an alter along with food, flowers, and candles to honor the dead.

Catalog No. 20598

Standing Coffin

This African coffin not only stands up, but it was likely never buried! Unlike many we see today, this coffin was carved out of wood in the shape of a tall man and may have been used as part of a funeral ceremony.

DISCOVER *Even More at a*
RIPLEY'S *Believe It or Not!*
Near You! VISIT RIPLEYS.COM

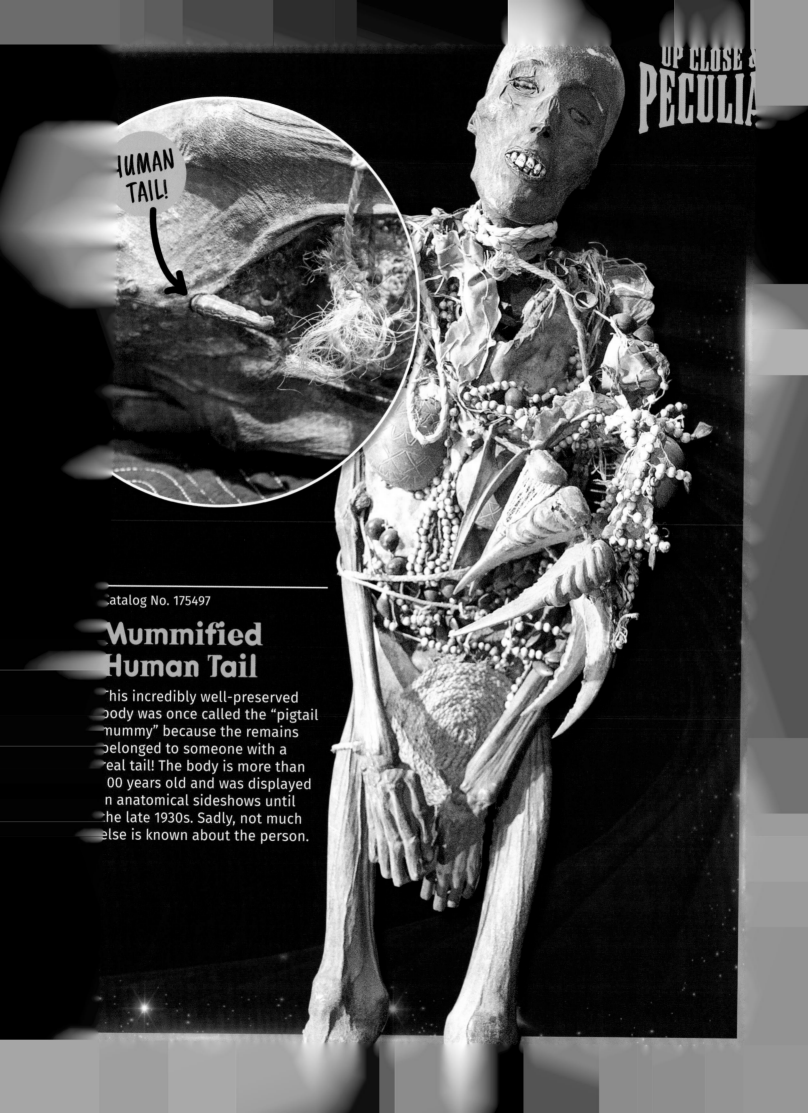

HUMAN TAIL!

Catalog No. 175497

Mummified Human Tail

This incredibly well-preserved body was once called the "pigtail mummy" because the remains belonged to someone with a real tail! The body is more than 00 years old and was displayed n anatomical sideshows until he late 1930s. Sadly, not much else is known about the person.

PARADISE LOST

This spooky abandoned ship was once a fancy hotel! Koh Chang Grand Lagoona Resort in Thailand was once a dream destination in the early 2000s. There, old boats like this one were turned into floating hotels! But it didn't last. It is not clear why the resort had to close. Some say there were money problems. Others say there were accidents on the boat's highest deck. Today, the ghost ship stands as a quiet reminder of what used to be.

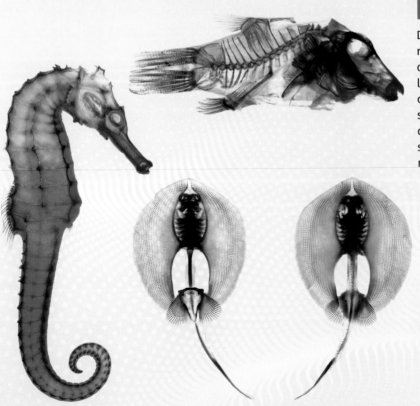

RADIANT REMAINS

Diaphonization is a process that turns animal remains into colorful works of art! Also called "clearing and staining," it requires a lot of training and involves the use of many chemicals. The animal is first soaked in a special liquid to make it see-through. Then, certain chemicals are used to add color to specific body parts, like bones or muscle. The result is a scientific masterpiece!

OPEN WIDE

If you thought pelicans couldn't get any weirder— they peli-can!

Pelicans have a large throat pouch for catching prey, kind of like a fishing net. But the pouch takes on an even stranger appearance when the bird yawns! Just like humans, birds need to stretch their bodies. One way to do this is by yawning. Pelicans yawn by opening their beak wide and rolling their head back. This inverts their pouch over their neck, creating a bizarre bulge in the shape of the bird's spine. Quite a show for an unsuspecting onlooker!

FISHY FEAST

A central African cichlid fish, known as Burton's mouthbrooder, shelters her eggs and baby fish in her mouth to keep them safe from predators—but sometimes eats more than three-quarters of them herself. The mother fish is unable to feed normally during the brooding period, so she snacks on her own young in order to remain healthy.

PURPLE HONEY

Honeybees in the Sandhills region of North Carolina produce purple honey. Flowers growing in the North Carolina coastal area contain more aluminum than other regions, and it's thought that the purple color of the honey is the result of a chemical reaction between acid in the bees' stomachs and the aluminum in the flowers on which they feed.

GREAT ESCAPE

The mystery of how a number of sheep kept escaping from their pen at a farm in Northumberland, England, was solved when a sheep named Lucy was caught on camera poking her head through the fence and opening the gate latch with her mouth.

OWL INTRUDER

A trespassing owl shut down Agnes Scott College's McCain Library in Decatur, Georgia, for four days in February 2023 after flying down the chimney and perching in the rafters 50 feet (15 m) above the floor and out of the reach of library staff. The bird was eventually captured and released by a falconer using a hydraulic lift.

ALWAYS STANDING

Giraffes spend most of their lives standing up. They even sleep and give birth while on all fours! The 6.5-foot (2-m) fall from the mother to the ground does not hurt a newborn giraffe.

PET TIGER

Pet cats share 95.6 percent of their genetic makeup with tigers.

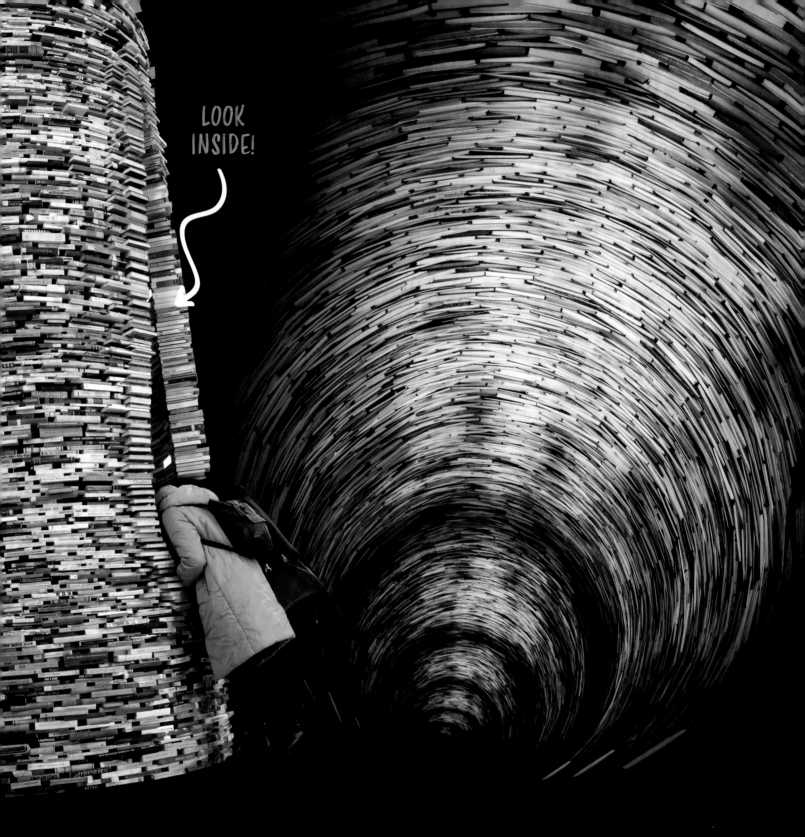

LOOK INSIDE!

BOUNDLESS BOOKS!

Artist Matej Krén used 8,000 books to build a tower that seems to stretch on forever!

Titled *Idiom*, the sculpture can be found at the Municipal Library of Prague in the Czech Republic. Matej used books that were going to be thrown away to create the tower. He gave them new life by turning them into immersive art. If you peer inside the tower's teardrop-shaped hole, the stack of books appears endless! Although it seems magical, it is actually a clever optical illusion. Matej created the effect by placing mirrors at the top and bottom of the tower!

WHEN CARS FLY

Built in the 1949, Moulton Taylor's Aerocar was a sight to be seen on the road and in the sky! Both a car and an airplane, the Aerocar featured detachable wings and a tail to quickly convert. On the road, it could go as fast as 67 mph (107 kmph), but in flight it could reach speeds of over 100 mph (161 kmph)! While sales did not take off due to cost and a compromised design, Taylor held on to the belief that the flying car would eventually become the norm!

LONG LINK
The Lake Pontchartrain Causeway, built across water in Louisiana, is so long that for eight of its 24 miles (38 km) you cannot see land in any direction.

NEIGHBORHOOD NOTE
The small town of Lewes in East Sussex, England, has its own currency—the Lewes pound—that can be used in local shops.

STEAMY SAUSAGES
A Finnish sausage called *makkara* is traditionally cooked over the hot stones in a sauna.

ROYAL WEE
A public bathroom in Rothesay, Scotland, displays a plaque with a coat of arms indicating which urinal was used by the then-Prince Charles when he visited.

NEW NAME
Deano Wilson, from Hampshire, England, legally changed his name to Fire Exit because he wanted to see his name in lights.

ZOMBIE VIRUS
Scientists at Aix-Marseille University in France revived a "zombie virus" that had been trapped in permafrost in a frozen lake in Yakutia, Russia, for 48,500 years.

COSMIC QUESTION

The James Webb Space Telescope is the largest and most powerful telescope ever launched into space. In June 2023, it captured something that really got people thinking! Images showed a strange shape in space that looked like a question mark. Scientists think it is likely the merger of two or more galaxies. Who knew punctuation could be so far out!

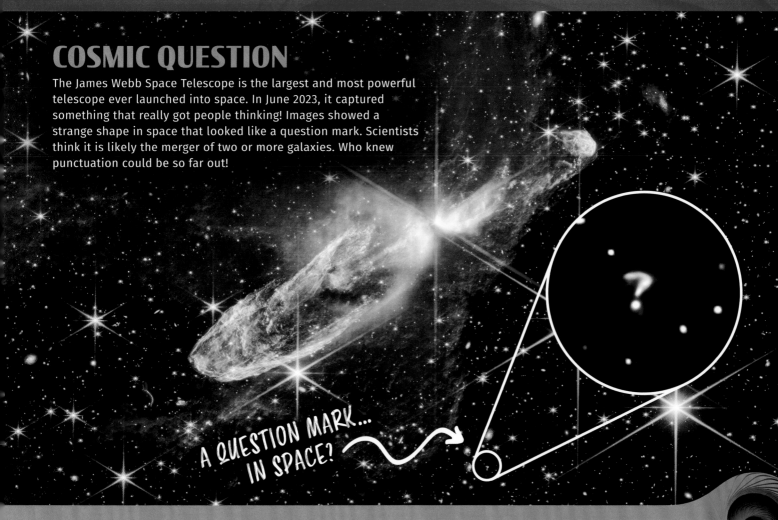

A QUESTION MARK... IN SPACE?

GOOD LUCK, HAVE FUN!

Relativity Space launched the world's first 3D-printed rocket into space! Called the Terran 1, the huge rocket was 85 percent 3D-printed and towered 110 feet (33 m) tall.

It soared into the sky from Cape Canaveral, Florida, on March 22, 2023. The mission—nicknamed GLHF for "Good Luck, Have Fun"—proved to be a big step for space travel. During its journey, the rocket made it through a point called "max q," where it was subjected to a large amount of pressure. This success shows that 3D printing can be used to make rockets, which might change how we explore space in the future.

3D-PRINTED ROCKET!

HAND PICKED

British artist Joe Black created a huge portrait of David Bowie out of 8,610 guitar picks! The artwork measures 6.5 feet (2 m) tall and took six weeks to finish. Sky Arts TV channel named David Bowie as Britain's most influential artist in the past 50 years and asked Joe to make the mosaic. Each pick has a shape that symbolizes the different arts Bowie impacted, such as music, film, and poetry. The portrait was given to a school in Bowie's old neighborhood, Brixton, to inspire future artists.

DR. DEEP SEA

University professor Dr. Joseph Dituri, a.k.a. Dr. Deep Sea, lived underwater for 100 days! He stayed at Jules' Undersea Lodge in Key Largo, Florida. He lived in a small habitat 22 feet (6.7 m) below the surface. Dr. Dituri wanted to see how the human mind and body handle being under extreme pressure for long periods. He ran experiments every day and shared his findings with students—all while submerged! Dr. Dituri's research will help scientists understand more about living in extreme places, such as the ocean and space!

Lunar LAKE

Colorful Coasts

Nature's colorful canvas stretches from coast to coast. Discover the different shades of sand around the world.

Black Beach: Covered in black volcanic ash and dark rocks, Reynisfjara is a popular black sand beach in Iceland.

Green Beach: Papakōlea Beach in Hawaii appears to have green sand thanks to tiny crystals called olivine.

Shaped like a quarter-moon and over 2,000 years old, Crescent Lake is an amazing sight in the Gobi Desert.

Near the city of Dunhuang, this oasis stands out with greenery against the desert sands. The lake is about 15 to 25 feet (4.5 to 17.6 m) deep despite being under a desert sun. Around the lake are small souvenir stalls and a traditional pagoda for tourists to visit. Crescent Lake shows how life can thrive even in the most deserted places.

Pink Beach: The pink beach on Komodo Island is one of seven in the world that gets its color in sunlight due to tiny organisms called foraminifera.

Red Beach: Rábida Island in the Galapagos is red! Its color comes from the iron in the volcanic rocks, called scoria, along its shore.

CRUSHED OYSTER SHELLS!

Catalog No. 14175

Oyster Elephant

Oyster shells can be crushed into a powder and made into an extremely hard building material. Crushed oyster shells are sometimes used to make household ornaments, like this unique elephant statue!

Catalog No. 6823

Shark Spine Cane

This walking cane is made from a shark's vertebrae! It once belonged to Robert Ripley, who enjoyed collecting canes made of unusual materials. Sharks have a soft skeleton made of cartilage, like your ears and nose.

Catalog No. 12892

Walrus Bladder Float

Arctic hunters use floats attached to harpoons to track prey in the water. Sometimes these floats are even made out of a walrus's bladder! The bladder's natural buoyancy ensures that the harpoon remains afloat, making it easier for hunters to locate and recover their spears after being thrown.

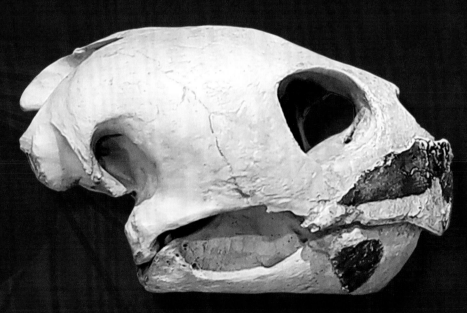

Catalog No. 167573

Sea Turtle Skull

The loggerhead is the largest hard-shelled sea turtle in the ocean. It can grow more than 3.5 feet (1 m) long and can weigh up to 400 pounds (181 kg)! Its big skull has extremely strong jaws—perfect for chowing down on tough-shelled prey, like clams and horseshoe crabs!

SHELL SHOCK

There's an underground cave in Margate, England, that is covered with seashells—around 4.6 million of them!

No one knows who made Shell Grotto or why. It was found by accident in 1835, but it was likely built a long time before that. Most of the shells are from creatures like oysters, whelks, and mussels that live near the Grotto. But some are from as far away as the Caribbean! Some people think Shell Grotto might have been an old temple, a secret meeting spot, or even just a fun hobby! No matter what it began as, today it is considered a work of art.

CONCH CASA

There's a home in Mexico shaped like giant seashells! Found on Isla Mujeres, Shell House is made up of different buildings. The largest is two stories tall and shaped like a conch shell. And the one right next to it looks like a hermit crab's shell! Brothers Eduardo and Octavio Ocampo came up with the idea for the home. They made it so there are almost no straight lines inside or outside!

SHELLBOUND

A plant collector in the 1800s turned a scallop into a book! Finding plants and pressing them between pages was a popular hobby in Europe during the Victorian era. These books were called herbariums. The person who made this one with a seashell cover clearly had a theme in mind. All of the plants inside are different kinds of seaweed!

BEND OVER BACKWARD

UK teen Liberty Barros can walk while bending her body so far backward that her head is by her knees! In 2022, at age 14, she made it 66 feet (20 m) in 22 seconds while in the position. And that's just one of Liberty's many flexible feats as a contortionist! She can also perform 11 chest-to-floor backbends in 30 seconds and tie her shoes in about 10 seconds while in the chest roll position.

THAT'S AN EXTREME BACKBEND!

LOOP, SWOOP, PULL... BEND!

KID UMPIRE
Nine-year-old Lathan Williams of Hammond, Louisiana, has been an umpire at local baseball games since he was five years old.

PUMPKIN PADDLE
Duane Hansen, from Nebraska, paddled 38 miles (60 km) down the Missouri River in a huge, hollowed-out pumpkin that he had grown himself. It took him 11 hours to complete the voyage crouched inside the 846-pound (384-kg) pumpkin, which he named Berta.

HIGH DUNK
Polish basketball player Piotr Grabowski soared into the air to complete a between-the-legs slam dunk at a height of 10.4 feet (3.2 m) in London, England. To enable him to perform the stunt, the hoop was raised 6 inches (15 cm) above the regulation NBA height.

TOES TARGET
Balancing on her hands, Shannen Jones used her feet to shoot an arrow at the center of a target from a distance of 60 feet (18.3 m). A professional contortionist, Shannen has been practicing foot archery for over six years. Known as the "Girl With No Bones," she is able to twist her entire body through a small hula hoop and solve Rubik's Cubes with her feet.

NO-SHOE STROLL
Fancy walking barefoot everywhere, even in the winter? Joseph DeRuvo Jr. from Connecticut has been doing just that for over 20 years. He started walking without shoes after getting painful bunions on his feet and says the experience has given him great sympathy for dogs because of the need to avoid sharp objects.

Spinning *Slain*

If you only have two hands, how can you spin 10 basketballs at once?

Using her entire body, Robyn Slain is one of only three women in the U.S. who can spin 10 basketballs at the same time! With patience and skill, she mesmerizes audiences with her dribbling, juggling, and spinning tricks on the court. But Robyn isn't new to basketball. She played in college at Southwest Baptist University in Missouri. Robyn now gives back to students around the country, challenging them to make positive choices and keep healthy habits.

CINEMATIC CITY

Furong Ancient Town in China is built on the cliffs of a nearly 200-foot-tall (61-m) waterfall!

The 2,000-year-old village looks like a scene out of a movie. In fact, a Chinese film called *Hibiscus Town* was filmed there in the 1980s! "Furong" means "hibiscus" in Chinese. The town used to be known as Wangcun, but it was renamed after the movie in 1997. Today, Furong is a quiet village but still gets many visitors. People love to walk around the town's old buildings and explore caves behind the waterfall. At night, bright lights cover the waterfall in beautiful colors!

EGG-AND-RUN RACE

Every year, the Italian town of Gandino stages a race between two people, one of whom has to run 7 miles (11.2 km) while the other picks up 100 raw eggs—one at a time—that have been placed in a line 3.3 feet (1 m) apart and deposits them in a container of sand back at the start point. The curious contest started as a bet between two friends in 1931, and the runner usually wins.

POOP TEA

Chu-hi-cha is a new type of tea brewed from caterpillar poop. It was developed by Tsuyoshi Maruoka, a researcher at Japan's Kyoto University, who, after feeding cherry tree leaves to gypsy moth larvae, noticed that the droppings that followed had a pleasant smell. So, he decided to brew them into tea and has since experimented with more than 40 types of plants and 20 different larvae.

TRUNK TIPPLE

Before it split, a baobab tree in Limpopo, South Africa, had a circumference of over 150 feet (46 m) and was so large that its cavernous hollows housed its own bar and wine cellar. The Sunland Baobab is more than 1,000 years old. Its tree bar was 13 feet (4 m) high from floor to ceiling and could accommodate 15 people.

NIGHT FLOWER

The Mexican "Queen of the Night" cactus produces its fragrant white flowers on rare occasions and only ever at night. The flowers wilt before dawn.

HOTEL HOP

It would take more than 400 years to spend a night in every one of the 150,000 hotel rooms in Las Vegas, Nevada.

NO BRIDGES

Even though the Amazon River is the world's second-longest river at 4,345 miles (6,992 km) long, there are no bridges spanning it.

LEEK LOVE

To celebrate the annual festival of St. John on the night of June 23, people in Porto, Portugal, take to the streets and hit each other with leeks or plastic hammers as a sign of affection.

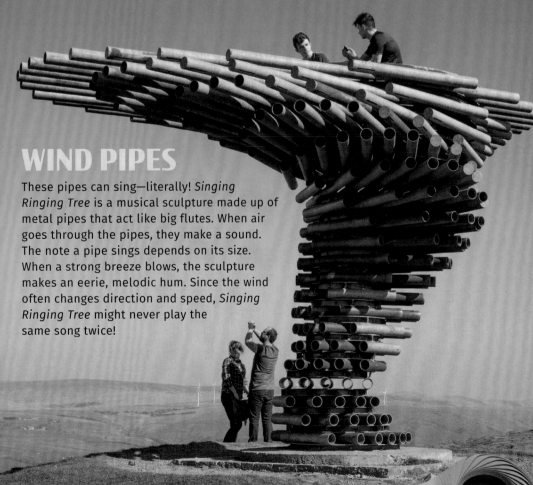

WIND PIPES

These pipes can sing—literally! *Singing Ringing Tree* is a musical sculpture made up of metal pipes that act like big flutes. When air goes through the pipes, they make a sound. The note a pipe sings depends on its size. When a strong breeze blows, the sculpture makes an eerie, melodic hum. Since the wind often changes direction and speed, *Singing Ringing Tree* might never play the same song twice!

TEMPLE HANGOUT

China's Horse's Hoof Temple complex is carved into the side of a mountain! The ancient site features dozens of caves connected by tunnels that were carved hundreds of years ago. They are home to both Chinese and Tibetan Buddhist temples. Inside, visitors can find hundreds of Buddha statues, old murals, and the reason behind the name "Horse's Hoof Temple." Kept safe within the cave walls is a rock with a strange marking. Legend says it was made by a winged horse that flew down from heaven and landed so hard it left a hoofprint in the stone!

JOUST ADD WATER

If jousting on horses isn't extreme enough for you, then check out water jousting!

In this version, jousters stand on a platform attached to the front of a boat. Each jouster holds a shield and a 9-foot-long (2.7-m) stick called a lance. The boats rush toward each other, and the rivals try to knock one another into the water with their lances! This sport of strength and balance dates back centuries to Ancient Egypt. Today, it is most popular in France.

CLOUD HAT

Lítla Dímun is a tiny island with its head in the clouds! It is one of the Faroe Islands—the smallest one, in fact. But Lítla Dímun still makes a big impression. It is often seen topped with one big cloud, as if wearing a hat! Moist air, wind, and the island's shape work together to create the humid headgear, proving even landmasses can make fashion statements.

LOST LENSES

Californian ophthalmologist Katerina Kurteeva removed 23 old contact lenses from the eye of a patient who had forgotten to remove them.

ROBOT RUNNER

A two-legged robot named Cassie, developed at Oregon State University, ran 328 feet (100 m) in 24.73 seconds at an average speed of 9 mph (14 kmph).

SPEEDY STEPS

Ganauri Paswan spent eight years carving more than 400 stone steps to a hilltop Hindu temple using only a hammer and chisel. The Baba Yogeshwar Nath temple in Bihar, India, was previously difficult to access because it is built on top of a steep 1,500-foot-high (457-m) hill. It used to take worshippers hours to reach the temple, but the steps have reduced the time to only 20 minutes.

FREEZER FLOAT

After his boat sank, Brazilian fisherman Romualdo Macedo Rodrigues survived for 11 days at sea in shark-infested waters by floating inside a freezer. Unable to swim, as the boat started to capsize and its contents scattered, he climbed into a large freezer that was bobbing on the water's surface and floated inside it until another boat picked him up off the coast of Suriname.

DUEL TO THE DEPTH!

"The hunt is part of the fun!

TITANIC COLLECTION

JD might be the world's biggest fan of the movie *Titanic*, and he has the VHS collection to prove it!

He has over 2,700 copies of the classic film and multiple dummies of Leonardo DiCaprio as the legendary Jack Dawson. To better understand his boatload of love for the iconic film, Ripley's reached out to JD to get the full scoop.

Q: How often do you watch Titanic?

A: *Titanic* on VHS is constantly playing in the T room. So, everyday, baby!

Q: How do you decide which copy to watch?

A: Most VHS tapes are stacked from the floor to the ceiling, so they aren't easily accessible. Luckily, we get tons of donations, so loose tapes are always on deck and each one is better than the last!

Q: Do you have any favorite copies?

A: VHS numbers 500, 1,000, and 1,997 are special to me. They mark milestones in our journey, and we've celebrated with each!

Q: What extremes have you gone to in order to get your hands on a copy of Titanic?

A: Once, I heard there were tons of *Titanic* tapes in Colorado, so we flew out, rented a car, and searched high and low. There is a pretty extreme amount of time spent looking through various yard sales and thrift stores, digging through bins, and often we end up empty-handed. The hunt is part of the fun, though!

NEVER LET GO!

EYE SPY

The Sphere in Las Vegas, Nevada, is a dome that can look like almost anything, even a giant eyeball! Outside is the Exosphere made up of about 1.2 million lights, each shining 256 million colors and ready to become anything you can imagine! Inside is a massive 16K LED screen, measuring 516 feet (157 m) in diameter and 366 feet (111 m) high—that's taller than the Statue of Liberty! The Sphere fits almost 20,000 people to enjoy concerts, movies, and sports, too.

DOGGIE DRIVER

A truck that hit two other vehicles in the parking lot of a Walmart store in Kilgore, Texas, was being driven by a dog. The dog had been waiting for its owners to return, and when its leash became entangled on the emergency brake, it set the vehicle in motion.

JUMBO HANGOVER

Two dozen elephants were found fast asleep on the ground in the Keonjhar district of India after getting drunk. They had broken large pots of mahua, a popular liquor in the region. Wildlife officials were called in to wake the slumbering elephants by loudly banging drums after villagers had been unable to rouse them.

MOUTHLESS MOTH

The Atlas moth, which lives in the tropical forests of southeast Asia, only lives for five days because it has no mouth and is therefore unable to feed. It devotes its short life to finding a mate.

TOOTH TREASURE

While wading in the waters of Chesapeake Bay on Christmas morning in 2022, nine-year-old Molly Sampson discovered a 5-inch-long (12.5-cm), 15-million-year-old megalodon tooth. Megalodon sharks grew to over 33 feet (10 m) long and were the largest fish ever to have ever existed.

ZOMBIE ROACHES

The dementor wasp from Thailand preys on cockroaches by injecting venom into the roaches' bellies, turning them into zombies. By then prodding the helpless cockroach with its antennae, the wasp guides its victim into a safe spot, where it is promptly eaten.

REEF RAVER

Clam-oring for attention, the saltwater bivalve known as the electric clam can put on a light show! Electric clams flash to confuse and scare away predators. It's not light, though! When in danger, they expose and quickly hide a white, shiny, reflective tissue. The back and forth motion creates the illusion of a flashing light!

LITE-BRITE
LIKE A
DIAMOND!

Catalog No. 169223

Lite-Brite Rihanna

Artist Rob Surette of Andover, Massachusetts, used 50,080 Lite-Brite pieces to make this portrait of Rihanna. The further you are from the artwork, the more detailed it appears!

Catalog No. 175551

"Purple Rain" Coat

Prince wore this purple satin coat during his stage performances of "Purple Rain!" The coat has a high collar, padded shoulders, and silver studs.

Catalog No. 175654

Stop-Motion Tree

This Christmas tree is a screen-used prop from *The Nightmare Before Christmas.* Because it is a stop-motion animated film, each frame is actually a photo of a real set. Over 100,000 photos make up the movie, and more than 100 artists worked for over three years to make almost everything you see on screen!

DAY *of the* DOGS

The Kukur Tihar festival takes the phrase "every dog has its day" to the next level!

Known as "day of the dogs," Kukur Tihar honors the special bond between dogs and humans. It is celebrated on day two of the five-day Hindu festival called Tihar. In Hinduism, it is believed dogs are messengers of the god of death. To stay on the god's good side, people spend the day worshipping dogs. The furry friends are blessed with red marks called tikas, dressed in flowers, and of course, given lots of tasty treats!

Although it is a slow walker, the echidna is great at digging, swimming, and climbing!

TINY EGG!

ECHIDNA YOU NOT

Compared to most mammals, the echidna seems like an alien species. Its body is covered in sharp, protective spines. It has a beak-like nose that can sense electricity. It has no teeth and slurps up insects with a 6-inch-long (15.2-cm) tongue. Instead of giving birth to live young, a mother echidna will lay an egg and keep it in a pouch on her belly until it hatches. On top of all that, it is one of Earth's oldest surviving species of mammal!

LONG-LIFE LIZARD

According to legend, a Texas horned lizard was sealed alive without food, air, or water in the courthouse of Eastland, Texas, for 31 years. The lizard was placed there in 1897 as part of a time capsule and when the courthouse was prepared for demolition in 1928, it was found alive. Old Rip the lizard became so famous that before his death 11 months later, he went on a national tour during which he was presented to President Calvin Coolidge.

COLOR CHANGE

The shell of the pink fairy armadillo from Argentina changes color according to the temperature of its body. The tiny armadillo, which is only 4 inches (10 cm) long, depends on a network of blood vessels to regulate its body heat. When it loses heat, its shell turns bright pink, but when it drains blood from the shell to keep heat in, the shell becomes paler.

WOODPECKER PANTRY

A determined pair of woodpeckers filled the walls of a house in Santa Rosa, California, with more than 700 pounds (318 kg) of acorns. Dozens of holes had been pecked in the walls and stuffed with enough acorns to fill eight garbage bags.

MONKEY BUSINESS

A capuchin monkey named Route called 911 from a zoo near Paso Robles, California. Deputies from the San Luis Obispo County Sheriff's Office went to investigate and found that although the call had come from the zoo's offices, no human there had made it. So they concluded that the emergency call was made by the monkey who had picked up the zoo's cell phone and pushed the buttons.

GLOBETROTTER GECKO

A pack of strawberries purchased in a supermarket in Manchester, England, contained a baby gecko that had traveled with the fruit 2,500 miles (4,000 km) from Egypt. After buying the strawberries, Nikata Moran put them in her fridge for two hours before she spotted the 1-inch-long (2.5-cm) stowaway. None the worse for its ordeal, the gecko was taken to a nearby reptile rescue center.

NOT EGGS-ACTLY

Fish eggs, or roe, are a common sight in sushi restaurants. Most people don't think twice about eating the tiny orange orbs on top their favorite rolls. But did you know that the reproductive cells of male fish can also be eaten? That's right—fried, steamed, or even raw, fish sperm sacs are considered a delicacy in Japan! Known as shirako or milt, it is said to taste rich, like butter, and a little bit sweet. When in season, the dish can be very expensive. Would you try this unique food?

EX-SQUEEZE ME, I'M COMING THROUGH!

TIGHT SQUEEZE

The Corinth Canal in Greece is a passageway that's so narrow, large ships need tugboats to lead them through! The canal is 3.9 miles (6.3 km) long and varies in width. It ranges from 69 feet (21 m) wide at the bottom to 82 feet (25 m) wide at the water's surface. The tight passage was completed in 1893, and up to 12,000 vessels travel through the canal every year!

SHIPPING STADIUM
Stadium 974 in Qatar, a venue for the 2022 World Cup, was built from 974 repurposed shipping containers so that it could be dismantled and reassembled in a new location after the soccer tournament ended.

NO NOISE
Whistling in the street for a taxi was banned in London, England, during World War I in case the sound was mistaken for an air raid warning.

SUNKEN SHIPS
Around 50 sailing ships are buried under the streets of San Francisco's financial district. As the city expanded rapidly in the second half of the nineteenth century, the shoreline of San Francisco Bay was built over, burying vessels that were abandoned in the harbor by men seeking their fortune in the 1849 California Gold Rush.

SECRET SNAKES

Calvin Bautista from New York City was caught smuggling three Burmese pythons in his pants at a border crossing between the U.S. and Canada. He rode on a bus with the snakes, which can grow to over 13 feet (4 m) long, making them among the world's largest.

SPACE PURSE
French luxury accessory brand Coperni created a $43,000 purse from a piece of meteorite that fell to Earth 55,000 years ago.

UNFORTUNATE NAME
From 1974 to 2003, the head of the Catholic Church in the Philippines was Cardinal Sin! Cardinal Jaime Sin would greet visitors by saying, "Welcome to the house of Sin."

SKIN CRAWL
A 64-year-old Spanish sewer worker developed such a serious parasitic roundworm infection that doctors could see the larvae crawling beneath his skin.

BUTTER RIVER
Firefighters called to a blaze at the Associated Milk Producers Inc. Plant in Wisconsin were hampered by a 3-inch-deep (7.62-cm) river of melted butter.

VOLCANO**VISION**

I spy with my... volcanic eye? For just a moment during its 2023 eruption, Iceland's Litli-Hrútur volcano looked just like an eye!

It spewed lava for almost a month, making this photo by explorer Gunnar Freyr Gunnarsson even more impressive. He had to be in the right place at the right time to capture the rare shot. His photos went viral when he shared them online. With its black sand eyelids and fiery lava iris, it made many people think of one eye in particular: the Eye of Sauron from *The Lord of the Rings* films. Luckily, the volcanic eye did not pose any threat to the people of Iceland (or Middle Earth).

PEANUT PUSHER

Bob Salem did something nutty—he pushed a peanut all the way up Pikes Peak in Colorado with his nose! It takes a strong hiker around eight hours to summit this 14,115-foot (4,302-m) mountain. Bob's odd adventure, in a nutshell, took him seven days! Using a spoon strapped to his face, he rolled his way to the summit. Strangely enough, Bob was not the first person to complete this challenge. He's actually the fourth! The last time was in 1976, making Bob the first person in the twenty-first century to push his peanut to the top!

THAT'S NUTS!

Turbo Charged!

The eSkootr Championship is the world's first race series for electric scooters!

The races see riders zipping around city streets on custom scooters at speeds of up to 60 mph (37 kmph)! The championship debuted in London in 2022. There, 30 racers from 10 national teams drove their scooters on a 1,542-foot-long (470-m) course with 12 turns. The event not only created a new sport, it also promoted a safe and sustainable way to travel that is kind to the planet. Everybody wins!

SCOOTING AT 60 MPH (37 KMPH)!

HAPPY FEET

Lucas, an African penguin at San Diego Zoo in California, can walk more easily after being fitted with a pair of padded neoprene and rubber boots. Lucas was diagnosed with a degenerative condition called bumblefoot, which causes painful lesions in birds' feet. Zookeepers encouraged him to walk across sand to make impressions of his feet. Using those, they created molds that a specialist company used to make the custom footwear.

SCORPION SURPRISE

After a trip to Croatia, a woman returned to her home in Natternbach, Austria, to find that 18 scorpions—a mother and 17 babies—had stowed away in her suitcase.

CANINE CONGA

German dog trainer Wolfgang Lauenburger taught 14 dogs to walk in a conga line together, all standing on their hind legs with their front paws resting on the dog in front. He has also trained one of his dogs, Balu, to jump rope on his hind legs and together the pair skipped over a rope 32 times in 30 seconds.

BEE BAIT

The bucket orchid plant of South and Central America has a clever way of spreading its pollen. It lures a bee with a sticky, aromatic liquid, into which the bee falls. The bee's only way to escape from the plant is through a narrow spout coated in pollen, which sticks to the bee's furry body—and when the bee is drawn to another bucket orchid, the pollen falls off and pollinates it.

FUNKY FEAST

Thorrablót is a traditional Icelandic mid-winter festival where they eat many delicacies including sour rams' testicles. The testicles are washed and then pickled for several months in whey before being sliced and served.

BENDY BORDER

Contrary to popular belief, Colorado's borders do not form a perfect rectangle. Instead, the state's marginally meandering borders give it 697 sides, making it a hexahectaenneacontakaiheptagon!

LONG BAR

The Humble Baron whiskey distillery in Shelbyville, Tennessee, has a bar 518 feet (158 m) long—the length of 6.5 tennis courts.

SLOW STRUCTURE

Germany's Cologne Cathedral took 632 years to build. Construction of the cathedral began in 1248, but it was not finished until 1880. At 516.4 feet (157.4 m), it was the tallest building in the world for four years, until the completion of the Washington Monument.

ROAD HOGS

Pigs still can't fly but at Pennywell Farm in Devon, England, they race! Every afternoon at Bacon Brook, miniature pigs compete to see who's the fastest. Spectators even get to pick the pig they think will win! After the race, fans can take photos and cuddle with the miniature pigs. A day of racing makes the speedy porkers hungry, so people can feed them, too!

ENLARGE *and* IN CHARGE

CAN YOU SOLVE ALL SEVEN?

An extreme close-up can make even the most common object look totally different. Can you identify these items? Look closely and read the clues—things are not always what they seem!

1. TO THE POINT

You can really leave a mark with this object! You will find one in almost every school, home, and business. It easily glides across paper and can be used to create anything from a love letter to a stick figure!

2. READY FOR TAKEOFF

You might see this object above you or find one outside on the ground. It comes in many shapes and colors. It gives its owner warmth, protection, and the power of flight!

3. IT'S ALIVE!

This fuzzy growth is formed by some fungi. There are thousands of different kinds! It can be found everywhere and spreads by air, water, or even animals. You might have seen it on food that has gone bad, like old bread.

4. PUT A RING ON IT

This object is one of the hardest materials on Earth! But don't think that means it doesn't have a soft side—this item is often used as a symbol of love! If you see one on someone's left ring finger, that usually means they are engaged or married!

5. ON SIGHT

If you were looking at this object in real life, it might be looking right back at you! It would also see everything to the left, right, and behind itself with its nearly 360-degree field of vision!

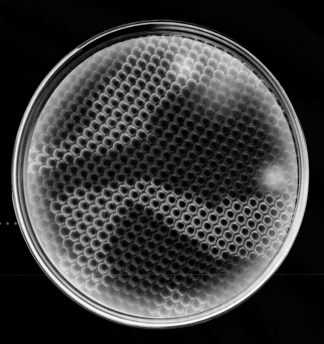

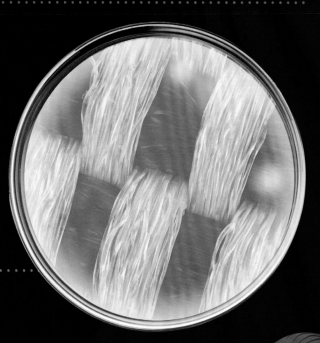

6. BRUSH UP

This item is found all over the human body and it clogs shower drains. Ripley's Believe It or Not! is the proud owner of a 225-pound (102-kg) ball named Hoss that is made of this object!

7. FEELING COZY

This object dates back at least 700 years! Today, many people make it as a hobby. It comes in many colors, sizes, and designs. It can be used to keep you warm, make you feel stylish, or both!

HOW DID YOU DO?

ANSWERS: 1. Ballpoint pen, 2. Bird feather, 3. Mold, 4. Diamond, 5. Insect eye, 6. Human hair, 7. Knitted fabric

THE GIANT'S CAUSEWAY

The Giant's Causeway on the coast of Northern Ireland has more than 40,000 rocks that fit together like puzzle pieces!

Perhaps their most striking feature is their shape. Almost all of them are six-sided hexagons! This is because they are a type of rock called columnar basalt, which is formed as hot lava cools down. The hexagon shape comes from the way the lava cracks as it hardens. Legend says the site was once part of a giant's path to Scotland and that one giant, named Finn McCool, ripped it all up, leaving what is seen today.

VIDEO VILLAGE
Around a third of the 3,000 people living in Tulsi, a small village in India's Chhattisgarh state, make YouTube videos for a living.

COUPLES CONFINEMENT
Couples in Biertan, Romania, whose marriages were on the rocks, used to be locked away by the local bishop in a matrimonial prison for up to six weeks to sort out their differences. The sparsely furnished cottage proved so successful that in 300 years there was only one divorce in the area.

INSECT ICES
Thomas Micolino's ice cream parlor in Rottenburg am Neckar, Germany, sells cricket-flavored ice cream served with a topping of dried brown crickets.

DRY COUNTY
Every drop of Jack Daniel's whiskey sold around the world is produced at the distillery in Moore County, Tennessee, which has been a dry county ever since prohibition, meaning it is illegal to purchase alcohol there. However, sampling whiskey in the distillery is permitted.

SURFING SANTA
At Mooloolaba, a coastal resort in Queensland, Australia, Santa traditionally shows up each Christmas wearing sunglasses and, instead of a sleigh, he arrives in a surf boat or parasails onto the beach.

CROSS COUNTRY
Robert Pope, from Liverpool, England, ran the width of Ireland in a day. He covered the 134 miles (215 km) from Galway City on the west coast to Dublin on the east in 23 hours 39 minutes.

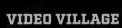

CARDIFF GIANT

The Cardiff Giant is often called "America's Biggest Hoax." In the 1860s, a man named George Hull hired sculptors to make a 10-foot-tall (3-m) statue. He then buried it on a farm in Cardiff, New York. On October 16, 1869, workers on the farm found the statue while digging a well. Some people believed it was a real giant that turned into stone. Others thought it was an ancient sculpture. Many came from far away and paid money to look at the Cardiff Giant. Even P. T. Barnum of circus fame tried to buy it! But just a few months after it was dug up, most agreed the statue was a fake and George Hull confessed to the hoax. Today, the Cardiff Giant is owned by the Farmers' Museum in Cooperstown, New York.

In 1948, a mock funeral was held for the Cardiff Giant.

LIGHT RAIL

An abandoned railway tunnel in Helensburgh, New South Wales, Australia, glows an eerie blue-green color at night after becoming home to a huge colony of thousands of glow worms.

NEWLYWEDS RESCUED

Newlyweds Panav and Victoria Jha missed their own wedding reception after being trapped in a hotel elevator for two and a half hours. The elevator had stopped between floors, so they and other members of their wedding party were winched to safety one by one.

DUMB MOVE

After being on the run for seven years, fugitive Thomas Ngcobo was finally arrested when he walked into a police station in Mpumalanga, South Africa, to apply for a job there.

2,310 NAMES

Lawrence Watkins, from Auckland, New Zealand, changed his name via deed poll and now officially has 2,310 first names. He chose names that were significant to himself and his family and they include Hannibal, Napoleon, Narcissus, and Sherlock.

MOOSE MISHAP

Former Norwegian soccer player Svein Grøndalen, who played 77 international games for his country, once had to miss a match after colliding with a moose while he was out on a training run.

TOUGH TEETH

Using just his teeth, Ashraf Mahrous Mohamed Suliman pulled a 34,679-pound (15,730-kg) truck in Ismailia, Egypt. One end of a strong rope was tied to the front of the truck and he held the other end between his teeth.

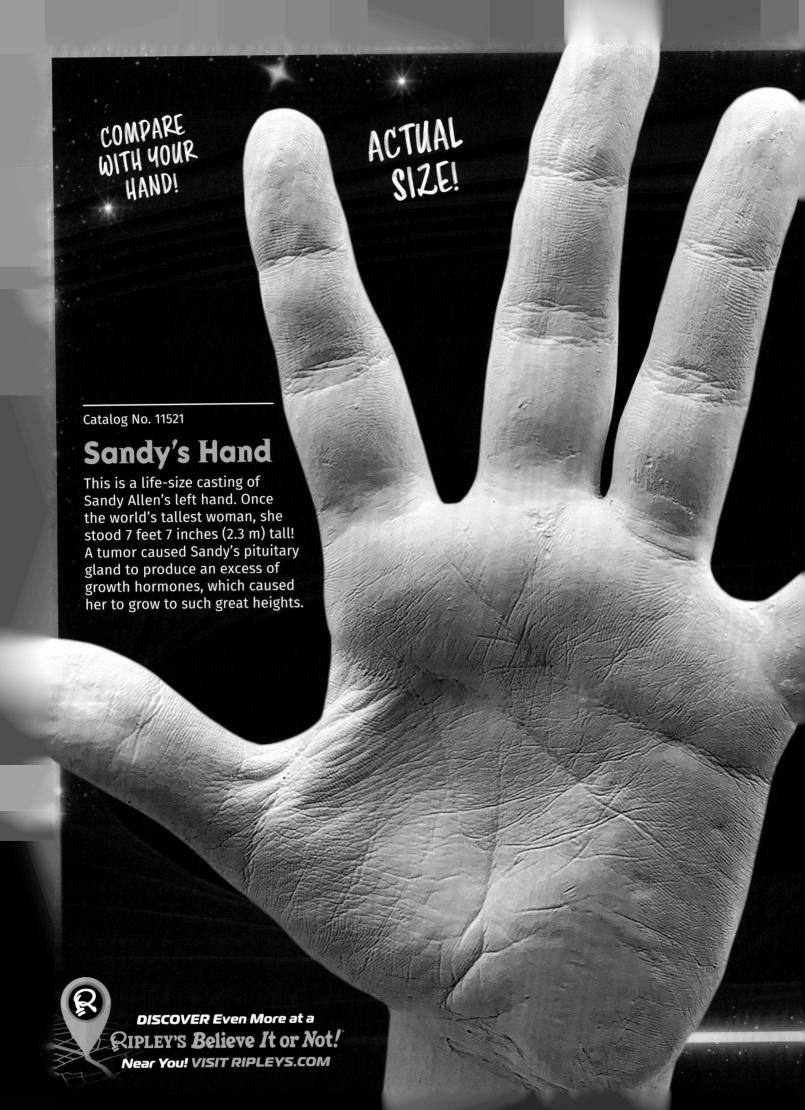

COMPARE WITH YOUR HAND!

ACTUAL SIZE!

Catalog No. 11521

Sandy's Hand

This is a life-size casting of Sandy Allen's left hand. Once the world's tallest woman, she stood 7 feet 7 inches (2.3 m) tall! A tumor caused Sandy's pituitary gland to produce an excess of growth hormones, which caused her to grow to such great heights.

Catalog No. 174563

Giant's Hammer

Jóhann K. Pétursson was the tallest Icelandic man on record! Known as the Viking Giant, he performed in European vaudeville theaters and North American circuses. For some of his performances, he would wear full Viking regalia and would carry a Viking war hammer, which is shown here.

Catalog No. 17900

Tire Shoes

These size 24 shoes are 16 inches (40.6 cm) long and made from recycled car rubber! They once belonged to Haji Alam Mohammad Channa, who held the title of the world's tallest man from 1982 to 1998.

BIG
SHOES TO
FILL!

MECH-ANIMAL *Kingdom*

The Machines of the Isle in Nantes, France, is an artistic playground where you can ride larger-than-life mechanical animals!

You can play with big birds, a huge spider, large ants, and even a four-story-tall elephant! The Grand Éléphant stands almost 40 feet (12 m) tall, stretches 26 feet (8 m) wide, and measures almost 70 feet (21 m) long. It can carry up to 50 passengers on a journey through the park. Inside, you can watch its gears move and listen to a guided tour about the metal creature. It even sprays water from its trunk!

Doggone Cute!

Scooter the dog may have a *ruff* time at a beauty contest, but he is a proud winner of the World's Ugliest Dog contest!

Despite its name, the contest celebrates all dogs and encourages people to adopt from shelters. In 2023, Scooter stole the judges' hearts. His wispy white hair, floppy tongue, and moving story earned the Chinese crested first place. Born with hind legs that face backward, Scooter was almost put down as a puppy. Thankfully, he was saved from that sad fate. More than seven years later, he now scoots around bringing love and joy to his owner, Linda Elmquist—and shows all who meet him that true beauty comes from within!

DING DONG

Bailey, an adopted husky mix dog who went missing from her new home, showed up two days later after walking 10 miles (16 km) to her former shelter in El Paso, Texas, and ringing the doorbell in the middle of the night.

BLOOD BLOCKS

During the hot Brazilian summer, some big cats at a zoo in Rio de Janeiro were given blood-flavored ice treats to keep cool. Black jaguars and lions were fed ice blocks that had been laced with a mixture of cow's blood, chicken, and minced meat.

SLIPPERY SNACK

The shoebill, a powerful African wading bird, stands at more than 4 feet (1.2 m) tall. With a wide beak that is over 8 inches (20 cm) long, it can easily swallow baby crocodiles and 4-foot-long (1.2-m) lungfish.

CAMEL CUSTOMER

Brandon Nobles of Nevada sometimes takes his 14-year-old rescue camel, Fergie, to an In-N-Out Burger drive-through restaurant in Las Vegas, where Fergie loves the french fries.

SURPRISE BIRTH

Momo the lar gibbon shocked workers at Japan's Kujukushima Zoo by giving birth in 2021, despite living alone in an enclosure with no males around. Two years later, DNA tests showed that the father was Itou, a male who lived in the adjoining enclosure. The gibbons had successfully mated through a 0.35-inch (9-mm) hole in a perforated partition board that separated the two enclosures.

HEART SONG

The male frigatebird wins the ladies over by wearing his heart on his sleeve! What looks like a bright red balloon on the seabird's chest is actually a flap of skin called a gular pouch. The male inflates it as a way to show off. And if the display doesn't catch a female's eye, the frigatebird will also play a song for her by clicking his beak and drumming on the air-filled pouch!

ABRA-CLAM LINCOLN

A 6-inch-long (15-cm) quahog clam weighing 2.6 pounds (1.2 kg) was found on the Florida coast in 2023—and it's 214 years old! By studying the bands on the clam's shell, scientists worked out that it was born in 1809, the same year as Abraham Lincoln. The clam was later released back into the Gulf of Mexico.

SELFIE SNAPS

A motion-activated camera set up to capture pictures of wildlife near Boulder, Colorado, was mainly used by a single bear—it triggered around 400 selfies in one night.

SCORPION ON ICE

Scorpions are able to cope with such extreme temperatures that researchers have frozen them overnight, then placed them out in the sun the following day and watched them thaw out and walk away unharmed.

FLYING FELINE

Security staff at New York's John F. Kennedy International Airport noticed an unusual item in the X-ray of a traveler's bag—a stowaway cat. The owner of the bag was preparing to fly to Orlando, Florida, unaware that the tabby cat named Smells had climbed into his suitcase and was planning to join him on the trip.

STEEP SHEEP

Prized for their tall stature and fine horns, Ladoum sheep are considered a mark of status in Senegal and a single animal can sell for up to $85,000, making one far more expensive than a new car.

UH, MOO?

THE COW'S MEOW

Moo-ve over, purebred kitties. The Thailand Cat Show has introduced a new event: the "Cats Who Look Like Cows" competition! More than 100 black-and-white cats entered in 2023. They were graded based on how much they looked and acted like cows. The winner? A chill feline named Arpo, whose fluffy fur and relaxed attitude left the judges in *udder* amazement.

Beautiful BLOOMS

During springtime, fields all over the Netherlands bloom with millions of tulips!

Tulips are native to central Asia, but didn't gain popularity until reaching the Netherlands. There, during a period of time in the 1600s known as Tulip Mania, they became the world's most expensive flower. They were said to have cost 10 times more than a worker's average salary in the Netherlands! Now, the country's most famous tulip landscape is Keukenhof garden. More than 7 million flowers are planted there each year!

BEJEWELED BRACELET

Noah Ost of Buffalo, New York, made a Taylor Swift friendship bracelet that measures 91.4 feet (27.9 m) long! The high school art teacher spent 20 hours threading beads to spell out the lyrics of their favorite Swift song, "All Too Well (10 Minute Version)." Once completed, the bracelet weighed 0.75 pounds (0.34 kg)! Rather than wear it, Noah opted to hang the friendship bracelet on their wall like garland.

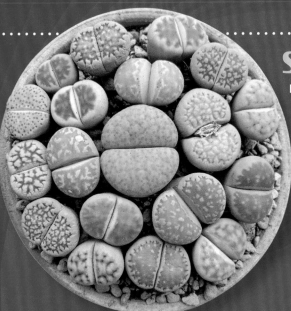

SUCCULENTS THAT ROCK

Lithops, also called living stones, are small plants found in southern Africa. They look like rocks, which helps them hide from animals that might want to eat them. These special plants have thick leaves that grow near the ground and make pretty flowers. They are also a popular houseplant!

THESE STONES ARE... ALIVE?

MILLIPEDE (TAYLOR'S VERSION)

Taylor Swift is one of the biggest names in music... and millipedes? Meet *Nannaria swiftae*, or the Swift twisted-claw millipede! It was found by bug expert (and Swiftie) Derek Hennen. Naming the leggy creature after Taylor Swift was his way of saying "thank you" for her songs. But the arthropod and pop star have more in common than their names. The millipede lives in Tennessee—the same state where Taylor Swift started her music career!

TOGETHER FOREVER

These two skeletons have been holding each other for about 6,000 years!

Called the "Lovers of Valdaro," they are named after the Italian village where they were found in 2007. It is believed the bones belonged to a man and a woman, both about 20 years old. No one is sure how the couple died, but there were no signs of a violent end. Some believe they may have frozen to death while holding each other. Others think the bodies were placed in the romantic position after they died. No matter how it happened, everyone agrees they should be kept together. Today, they are on display in Italy's National Archaeological Museum of Mantua.

PLANT PALS

Moss Amigos are pet plants with personality! Started by Jared Oliva and Will Starr, Moss Amigos lets you turn a floating ball of algae, or marimo, into a fun friend. You get to choose a size and the kind of stones in its jar. You can even give it a cute little hat! All your Moss Amigo needs to stay happy is a shady spot, fresh water, and a little love. Talk about a low-maintenance pet!

EARLY INVENTION
The pepper grinder was invented by the French company Peugeot in 1842—about 50 years before they became known for producing cars.

HAIRY HAZARD
Several gardens in Bradford, England, were flooded after someone threw two toupees down a drain, blocking it, and causing sewage to overflow.

SNAIL MAIL
A letter written and mailed in Bath, England, in 1916 was finally delivered to its destination, a London apartment, in 2023—107 years late.

SPECTACULAR SOAP
Russian soap artist Yulia Popova crafts bars of soap to look like chocolate desserts and tasty fruits such as peaches, strawberries, and blackberries.

EARLY MEDALS
The winners at the first modern Olympic Games in 1896 received silver medals. Gold medals were not introduced until 1904.

DOUBLE WIN
On November 9, 2022, Brenda Gomez Hernandez won $100,000 through the state lottery on the same day that she gave birth to a baby girl.

SCALY SUPPORT

Joie Henney has an emotional support animal unlike any other—an alligator! The Pennsylvania man rescued Wally Gator in 2015, and the two have been best friends ever since! Joie knew Wally was special from the first time they met. Unlike other alligators Joie has helped rescue, Wally did not try to bite. In fact, he seemed to enjoy being held! Today, the two do everything together. Wally was even by Joie's side during his radiation treatment for cancer. People seem to love Wally wherever he goes. The reptile is well-behaved and wears a harness and leash.

HAVE YOU HUGGED AN ALLIGATOR TODAY?

Believe it or not, the visual appearance of Alligator Loki in the show *Loki* was based on Wally!

SEWER SURPRISE!

Plunging 164 feet (50 m) below London, England, is Loo Gardens—a floral art oasis deep inside London's "super sewer."

From a mini-rainforest to firs and twisting ivy, the garden's hand-crafted creations represent plant life native to London's Thames riverbank, which is expected to return in greater numbers once the sewer is fully active. There are even flowers made from recycled waste found along the river! Once complete, the sewer that the Loo Garden is temporarily flourishing in will prevent millions of tons of raw sewage from entering the River Thames every year.

WHAT A LOO-VELY SIGHT!

MASTER OF DISGUISE

The ghost pipefish just might be the king of camouflage! This amazing sea creature can almost disappear completely. This is thanks to how the colors, patterns, and textures of its skin match up perfectly with its environment. Some ghost pipefish even have partially see-through bodies, making them even harder to spot in the wild!

WHERE ARE YOU?

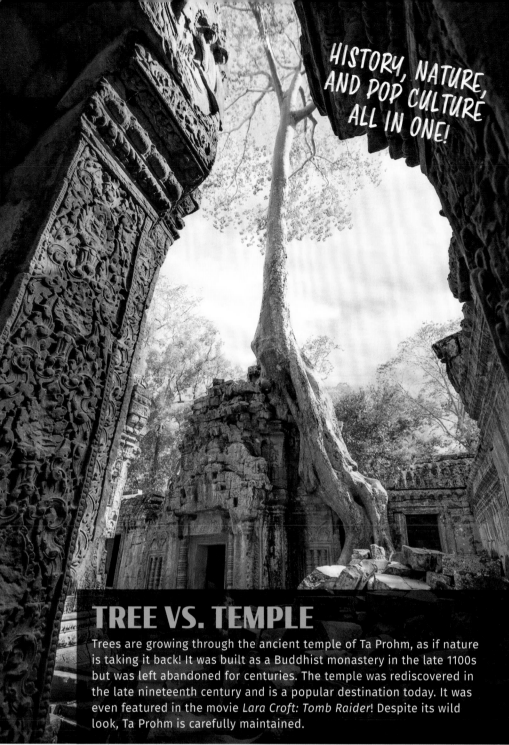

TREE VS. TEMPLE

Trees are growing through the ancient temple of Ta Prohm, as if nature is taking it back! It was built as a Buddhist monastery in the late 1100s but was left abandoned for centuries. The temple was rediscovered in the late nineteenth century and is a popular destination today. It was even featured in the movie *Lara Croft: Tomb Raider*! Despite its wild look, Ta Prohm is carefully maintained.

YOUNG GRADUATE

David Balogun graduated high school at age nine—half the age of normal graduates. He started at Reach Cyber Charter School in Harrisburg, Pennsylvania, as a third-grader and was awarded his high school diploma after completing the necessary studies virtually from his home in Bensalem.

NATIVITY SCENES

Michael Zahs, from Washington, Iowa, has a collection of more than 2,500 nativity scenes, which he has been gathering since the 1950s. His miniature scenes of Mary, Joseph, and the baby Jesus come from over 100 different countries and are made from a variety of different materials, from traditional wood to the more unusual yak wool and corn stalks.

SWIFT COURSE

In 2022, students at the University of Texas in Austin were able to study the songwriting of Taylor Swift as a literature course alongside the works of William Shakespeare, Geoffrey Chaucer, and Samuel Taylor Coleridge.

COCONUT SMASH

Indian martial artist K. V. Saidalavi used martial arts weapons called nunchucks to smash 68 coconuts in one minute—while the fruits were resting on the heads of volunteers.

KEEP IT REAL

For authenticity, Rockstar Games hired real-life gang members to voice background characters in the video game *Grand Theft Auto V*.

TRAILER DEMAND

Before *Star Wars: Episode I – The Phantom Menace* was released in 1998, fans were so keen to watch the film's first two-minute trailer that they bought tickets for other movies just to see the trailer—and then left the theater before the main movie began.

Surf & Turf

Mrs. Chook the chicken is making waves with her unlikely hobby—surfing!

This radical bird is owned by Elaine Janes of Victoria, Australia. Every day, she takes Mrs. Chook to Ocean Grove Beach for surfing lessons! The chicken enjoys swimming in the water, too. Elaine wanted more for her feathered friend than just a backyard life. Now, Mrs. Chook's ocean outings are a hit with the locals and beachgoers!

SURFING CHICKEN!

CLEVER CAMO

The orange oakleaf butterfly of southeast Asia looks and acts just like a dead leaf! When threatened by a predator, it starts to fly around wildly. Then, it falls into a tree and stays still with its eyes and wings closed. The veining on its closed wings looks exactly like a dry leaf. They even have white spots that resemble mold!

DEAD LEAF?

IN THE SPOTLIGHT

In 2023, Brights Zoo in Limestone, Tennessee, welcomed a baby giraffe that was born without spots! She was given the name Kipekee, which means "unique" in Swahili. And she earned it! She was the first spotless giraffe born since 1972. And for a little while, she was thought to be the only one in the world. But against all odds, another spotless baby giraffe was spotted in the wild in Namibia mere weeks after Kipekee's birth!

HAVE YOU SEEN MY SPOTS?

TOAD-ALLY HUGE!

TOADZILLA

Australian park ranger Kylee Gray found a cane toad that weighed a whopping 6 pounds (2.7 kg)! Six times larger than average, the amphibian was given a fitting nickname: Toadzilla. Kylee described it as "a football with legs." Unfortunately, cane toads are invasive. They were brought to Australia in 1935 and have caused major problems for native species ever since.

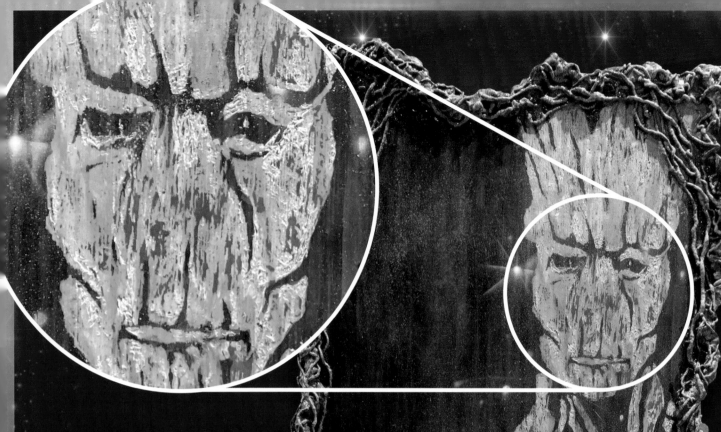

Catalog No. 175800

Pressure-Washed Groot

Sam Ward of New Braunfels, Texas, created this portrait of Groot by blasting layers of paint off a wooden board with a pressure washer! After featuring his sidewalk art in our book *Ripley's Believe It or Not! Level Up*, we invited Sam to the Ripley's Headquarters in Orlando, Florida, to make this custom piece for us. Unlike his sidewalk art, this piece is portable and can be displayed at any Ripley's Believe It or Not! location around the world!

DISCOVER *Even More at a*
RIPLEY'S *Believe It or Not!*

Catalog No. 174602

Psycho Door

This door was used for shots of Norman Bates's house in the iconic horror movie, *Psycho*. Adding to the grim nature of this piece, the owner of the Dallmann-Kniewel Funeral Home in Rib Lake, Wisconsin, purchased the door in the early 2000s and installed it as the front door of the business. It was also in Wisconsin where notorious killer and body snatcher Ed Gein committed the unspeakable acts that inspired the novel on which the film was based!

Catalog No. 167660

Rubik's Cube Joker

This rendition of Heath Ledger as the Joker is created entirely from 336 Rubik's cubes! Artist David Alvarez has made other portrait mosaics in the Ripley collection out of Post-t notes, dice, and even playing cards!

Funky Fungi

Mushrooms come in countless shapes, sizes, shades, and even smells! Sometimes they're delicious, and sometimes they're deadly—which is why you don't eat any you find outside. Most of the time, they're just plain weird. Here are just a few of the strange fungi living among us!

BASKET STINKHORN

This fungus is nothing like your typical toadstool. Also known as the red cage or latticed stinkhorn, *Clathrus ruber* kind of looks like a hollow, red soccer ball. The inside is covered in slime and filled with the mushroom's spores. The slime smells like rotting flesh! Flies are drawn in by the stench and land on the slime. When they fly off, some spores go with them and spread to where the flies land.

STINKY SOCCER BALL!

AMETHYST DECEIVER

A purple mushroom sounds like something out of a fairy tale. Even the name "amethyst deceiver" has a fantasy feeling to it. But *Laccaria amethystina* can be found in real life, and it's usually among piles of dead leaves. Its violet hue is most vibrant when the mushroom is young and damp. When the air is dry and as the fungus gets older, its color turns pale from the top-down.

GIANT PUFFBALL

This mushroom could double as a volleyball! *Calvatia gigantea* normally grows 8 to 20 inches (20 to 50 cm) wide, but it can get even larger. In 1987, a giant puffball mushroom measuring more than 8 feet (2.4 m) wide and weighing almost 50 pounds (23 kg) was found in Quebec, Canada! Many professional mushroom hunters love this edible species, as it can be sliced into giant slabs like a steak!

DOUGH FUNGI?

BRAIN MUSHROOM

The reddish-brown cap of *Gyromitra esculenta* looks like a human brain! But that doesn't mean it has your best interests in mind. Also called a false morel, the brain mushroom looks similar to an edible type of fungus. But it can be deadly poisonous when eaten. Talk about food for thought!

LOOKS LIKE TINY EGGS!

BIRD'S NEST FUNGUS

This isn't a bird's nest—it's a mushroom! Found all over the world, fungi in the Nidulariaceae family eat decaying matter such as dead trees, fallen leaves, mulch, and even animal poop! Instead of baby birds, their "eggs" contain millions of mushroom spores. When it rains, drops of water send the egg-like sacks flying through the air so the spores can spread to new places.

The LAST of CRUST

One House Bakery in Benicia, California, made a "clicker" monster out of bread!

The shop's owners, mother-daughter duo Hannalee and Catherine Pervan, were inspired by the TV show *The Last of Us*. Their zombie-like clicker stands in front of a fungi-covered wall, also made of bread. Titled "The Last of Crust," the sculpture took more than 400 hours to make and includes more than 1,000 bread mushrooms! To make the fungi, the team wrapped inflated balloons in dough. Once baked, the balloons were popped and removed. This was not One House Bakery's first bread sculpture! They make one every year for a local contest. Past sculptures have been based on fan favorites such as *Star Wars* and *Loki*.

MAMMO MIA!

Feast your eyes! In 2023, an Australian food company, Forged, grew a woolly mammoth meatball in a lab! But how did they do it? Most mammoths went extinct more than 10,000 years ago! Despite this, mummified mammoths have been found in places like Canada and Siberia. To make the meatball, genetic information from those remains was combined with elephant DNA. (Elephants are the closest living relatives to mammoths.) The mix was put inside a sheep cell, which multiplied into a big hunk of meat! Sadly, or perhaps thankfully, the meatball was just made for show. Scientists weren't sure it was safe to eat. It contained proteins that humans haven't eaten for thousands of years! And while no one tasted the giant meatball, some did smell it as it was cooked. Would you believe it? It smelled good!

GET THE PASTA!

CAR CHEAT
Ultramarathon runner Joasia Zakrzewski was stripped of her third-place medal in a 50-mile (80-km) race from Manchester to Liverpool, England, after it emerged that she had traveled by car for part of the race. Organizers became suspicious when they analyzed GPX data and saw that she had reached a speed of 35 mph (56 kmph) over part of the course, making her faster than Usain Bolt.

WALKING DEAD
Zhuo Kangluo was found alive and well nine years after it was thought he had been cremated. Family and friends thought they had identified his body after a car crash, and the body was cremated. But in 2023, he stunned them by wandering into a village near Chongqing, China.

GUARDS FOOLED
César Ortiz escaped from a jail in Asunción, Paraguay, by walking through the front gate disguised as a woman. His long hair wig, fake eyelashes, lipstick, fake fingernails, and women's clothes fooled the guards at several checkpoints.

LOTS OF LAYERS
Nineteenth-century British aristocrat Sir Tatton Sykes used to wear up to eight coats at a time, all of slightly different sizes. He liked to maintain a constant body temperature. When he felt too warm, he would remove one layer and allow it to fall to the ground. Local boys would collect his discarded coats and return them to his Yorkshire home for a small reward.

SKY-HIGH SANDALS
A pair of Steve Jobs's brown suede sandals sold at auction in 2022 for $218,750. He wore them at his home in Los Altos, California, where he co-founded Apple. The footbeds of the sandals still retain the imprint of his feet.

SKIPPED WEDDING
Soccer player Mohamed Buya Turay did not attend his own wedding in Sierra Leone because he was finalizing his transfer to Swedish club Malmö. He asked his brother to stand in for him at the ceremony, and the wedding pictures show his brother cutting the cake with the bride.

DISRUPTIVE DISORDER
Joanna Cox once slept for four whole days. She suffers from idiopathic hypersomnia, an unusual disorder that causes her to sleep for up to 22 hours a day. The condition has often caused her inconveniences, such as missing flights.

QUICK BLOOD
A red blood cell only takes about 20 seconds to travel all the way around your body.

Gold TO MOLD

Artist Kathleen Ryan breaks the mold with *Bad Fruit*!

She individually places thousands of sparkling gemstones, minerals, and beads to create large sculptures that look like moldy fruit. To create a 30-inch-wide (76-cm) lemon, it can take her up to two months and 10,000 beads. Some of her creations are 7.5 feet (2.3 m) wide!

7.8 FEET (2.4 M) LONG!

SECRET INGREDIENT

A waitress at a café in Hokkaido, Japan, was fired after being accused of mixing her own blood into the cocktail drinks she served to customers.

BAT SALIVA

Draculin, an anticoagulant used in medicine to prevent blood clots, is found in the saliva of vampire bats.

MOVIE MAGIC

Dane Grant and Dayna Porter, the stunt doubles for Tom Hardy and Charlize Theron on the movie *Mad Max: Fury Road*, fell in love while making the film and later married.

BUSHY BEARD

Joel Strasser from Idaho can fit 2,470 Q-tips in his bushy beard. It took him two hours to put the cotton swabs in position.

DRY DIET

A kangaroo rat can go its entire life without ever needing to drink a single drop of water. The rodent, which is native to the deserts of North America, can live for up to 10 years and survives by eating seeds and beans that have high water content. The rat has extremely efficient kidneys that enable it to produce concentrated urine in small amounts, and so it only passes a few drops of pee each day.

CAN CHOMP
René Richter from the Czech Republic used his teeth to bite 36 water-filled aluminum drink cans in half in one minute.

CALORIE COUNT
As well as the distance to the destination, pedestrian walking signs in Thessaloniki, Greece, also show how many calories you would burn by walking there.

COCONUT CRAZE
Balakrishnan Palayi, from Kasaragod, India, says he has eaten nothing but coconuts for more than 28 years to treat a disease that caused him to vomit whenever he ate.

ANCIENT CHEESE
In 2022, Archaeologists in Egypt discovered clay pots containing 2,600-year-old blocks of white halloumi cheese.

WATERMELON WHACK
Spanish athlete Roberto Rodriguez used his open hand to smash 39 watermelons in one minute.

DANCE DISASTER
While training for her role as a ballerina in the film *Black Swan*, American actress Natalie Portman's toenails fell off and she dislocated a rib during a lift.

Red Panda

You're not going to want to miss this un-*bowl*-ievable show!

Rong Niu, also known as Red Panda, performs amazing tricks on a unicycle! She does so while flipping bowls onto her head! Red Panda, from China, got her big chance to perform during halftime at a Los Angeles Clippers game in 1993. Her performance got an amazing response! Her act involves riding a 7-foot-tall (2.1-m) unicycle all while catching and balancing multiple ceramic bowls on her feet and head! Red Panda's amazing performances have made her an international star!

AMAZING FOCUS AND BALANCE!

THREE-POINTERS

On December 8, 2022, the Grinnell College men's basketball team from Iowa deliberately only attempted three-point shots during their game against Emmaus Bible College. They tried 111 three-pointers over the course of the game and scored 40 of them. The remaining points in their 124-67 victory came at the free throw line.

EYE POPPER

Sidney de Carvalho Mesquita from Brazil can pop his eyes 0.71 inches (1.8 cm) beyond his eye sockets. He discovered his unusual talent at age nine while making funny faces in the mirror. He can pop them out for up to 30 seconds at a time, during which he briefly loses his ability to see before his eyes can re-focus.

JAWS DROPPING

Twelve-year-old Campbell Keenan, from Southampton, Massachusetts, caught a great white shark that weighed over 400 pounds (181 kg) while fishing on a charter boat off the coast of Fort Lauderdale, Florida. It took over 45 minutes for him to reel in the 11-foot-long (3.4-m) shark with help from the boat's crew. The shark was then released back into the ocean.

ONE-WHEEL WONDER

Wesley Williams, from Weston, Florida, built and rode a 31.8-foot-tall (9.7-m) unicycle—only a year after breaking his back on a Spanish TV show where he fell 27 feet (8.2 m) to the floor when his previous unicycle malfunctioned. His injuries required five surgeries. He received his first unicycle as a Christmas present when he was six years old.

MINI GOLF

Cole Hetzel, his father Chris Hetzel, Tony Centers, and Bob Schoettinger played 2,097 holes of miniature golf in 24 hours at Putt-Putt Golf in Erlanger, Kentucky. The quartet played 116 rounds, walked nearly 20 miles (32 km), and took a combined 14,664 strokes.

UNIQUE MOVES

U.S. champion gymnast Simone Biles has five gymnastic moves named after her—two on the floor, one on the beam, and two on the vault.

STROLLER SPECTACLE

A father to quintuplets, Chad Kempel now has one more reason to be proud. He set a world record for running a half marathon while pushing his five youngest children in a stroller! With his wife, Amy, biking beside him, the family crossed the finish line in 2 hours 19 minutes at the Oakland Running Festival in California. He was pushing 240 pounds (108.86 kg), the combined weight of the stroller and children!

RUN, DAD, RUN!

ROLL OUT!

When the going gets tough, the tough get... rolling? At least, that's what the armadillo lizard of South Africa might say! When this reptile gets scared, it bites its own tail and curls into a ball. Its back, legs, neck, and tail are covered in thick spikes. When the lizard is rolled up, they help protect its soft underside from hungry predators.

ROCKABYE BABY

If you see a giant baby sleeping in the Gobi Desert, don't wake him up! The baby is actually a sculpture by artist and professor Dong Shubing titled *Son of the Earth*. It was created using 3D scanning technology. The peaceful sleeper is made of rough red sandstone, measuring almost 50 feet (15 m) long and over 14 feet (4.3 m) tall!

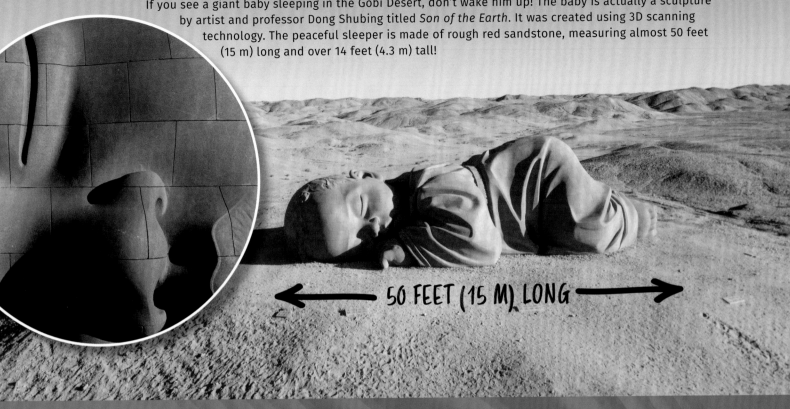

← 50 FEET (15 M) LONG →

KEPT CAKE

Elaine Nishimura made a surprising discovery after her mother died in 2019, aged 102. When going through her mother's things, Elaine found the top tier of her parents' wedding cake from 1943. The 76-year-old cake was in pristine condition and may be donated to a museum.

WEATHER WATCHER

In 2023, 92-year-old Arlene Cole of Newcastle, Maine, marked 65 years of serving as a weather watcher for the National Oceanic and Atmospheric Administration. Every day at 5 p.m., she reports on her local weather conditions

SPEED CLAPPER

Dalton Meyer, of Davenport, Iowa, can clap his hands 1,140 times in one minute—about 19 claps per second. He has mastered the art of wrist clapping, where he strikes the palm of his hand with his wrist and fingers.

BAR CRAWL

Nathan Crimp had a drink at 67 different bars in his hometown of Brighton, England, in 17 hours, starting at 11 a.m. on September 17, 2022, and finishing the following day at 4 a.m. He walked over 18 miles (29 km) and said a lot of his time was spent going to the toilet.

LAND HOPPING

It took Dr. Ali Irani and Sujoy Kumar Mitra from India just 3 days 1 hour 5 minutes to visit all seven continents of the world. They set off from Antarctica on December 4, 2022, and finished in Melbourne, Australia, on December 7.

NAP POD

In Japan, you can take a nap standing up! Made by Koyoju Plywood Corporation, Giraffenap is a vertical pod meant for standing sleepers. The Nescafe Sleep Café in Tokyo offered the standing sleeping pods for a limited time, and people paid to take naps in them! They have adjustable lights, armrests, and fans inside as well. The Giraffenap can also be used for tired workers in the office!

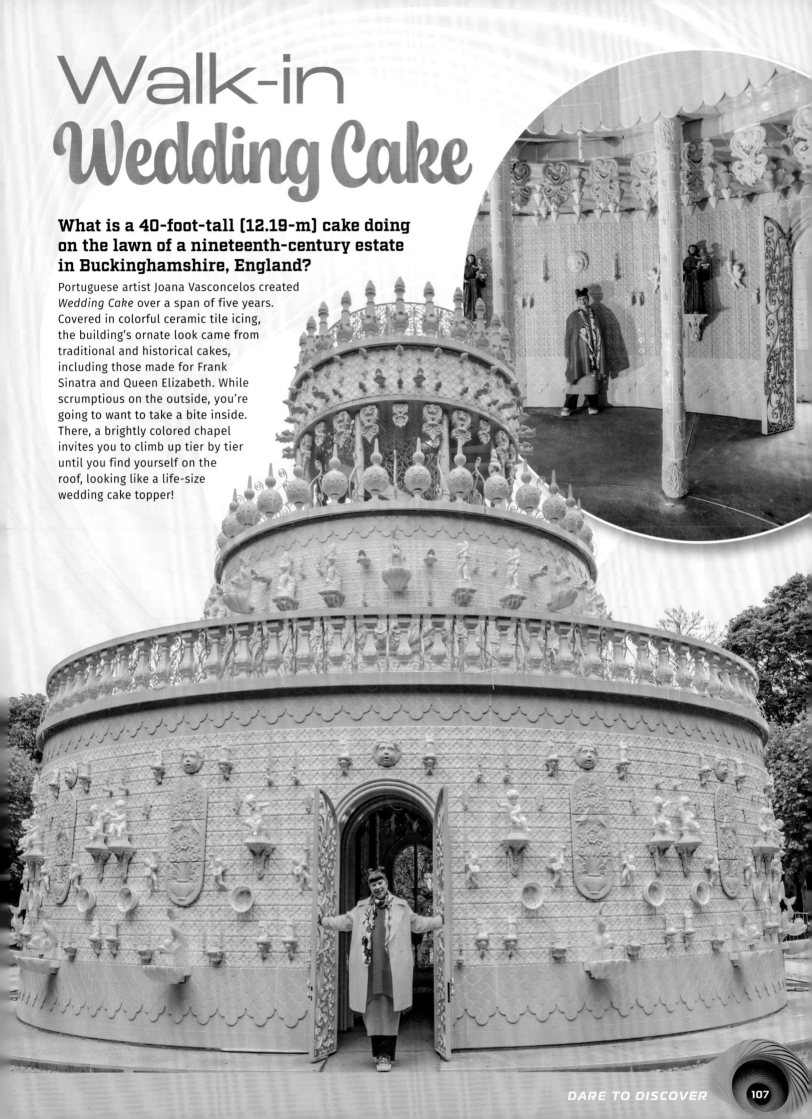

Walk-in Wedding Cake

What is a 40-foot-tall (12.19-m) cake doing on the lawn of a nineteenth-century estate in Buckinghamshire, England?

Portuguese artist Joana Vasconcelos created *Wedding Cake* over a span of five years. Covered in colorful ceramic tile icing, the building's ornate look came from traditional and historical cakes, including those made for Frank Sinatra and Queen Elizabeth. While scrumptious on the outside, you're going to want to take a bite inside. There, a brightly colored chapel invites you to climb up tier by tier until you find yourself on the roof, looking like a life-size wedding cake topper!

General Tom Thumb

Reaching just 3 feet 4 inches (1 m) tall, General Tom Thumb was once one of the world's most famous performers and even met the Queen of England three times!

Born as Charles Sherwood Stratton on January 4, 1838, he joined P. T. Barnum's circus at just four years old. There, Charles learned how to sing, dance, and more. His immense talent and small stature drew huge crowds. Charles, a.k.a. General Tom Thumb, was soon a worldwide celebrity. Check out these exhibits collected by Ripley's to get a fascinating glimpse into his life!

THESE BOOTS ARE MADE FOR PERFORMING!

TOM THUMB AND LAVINIA WARREN

Catalog No. 173793

Leather Boot

At 3 feet 4 inches (1 m) tall, Tom Thumb didn't require much leather to keep his feet covered! His boot measures 6.5 inches (16.5 cm) tall and 4.5 inches (11.4 cm) wide. Tom proved it's not the size of the shoe that matters, but the quality of the person in them.

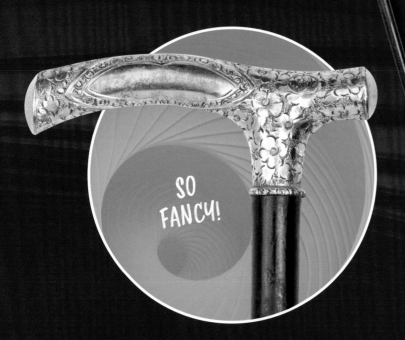

SO FANCY!

Catalog No. 173794

Walking Cane

This Victorian-era walking cane was owned by Tom Thumb and measures just 14.75 inches (37.5 cm) long! The cane is equipped with an ornate handle that makes it hard to miss despite its size.

Catalog No. 168342

Wedding Items

In 1863, Tom Thumb married the equally small Lavinia Warren. Lavinia worked as a performer for P. T. Barnum. The marriage was a major event in New York society. The happy couple stood on top of a grand piano in New York's Metropolitan Hotel to greet 2,000 guests at the reception. President Abraham Lincoln even hosted the couple on their honeymoon!

TOM THUMB'S GLOVE

LAVINIA'S STOCKING

WEDDING ALBUM LOCKET

Micro Crochet

Artist Lucia Dolgopolova makes micro-crochet animals as tiny as she possibly can—some as small as 0.04 inches (1 mm) tall!

Her crochet creatures are even smaller than the thickness of a U.S. penny! To achieve these tiny sizes, Lucia uses thin thread instead of thick yarn. Amazingly, she doesn't use a magnifying glass! She says it's to give herself a fun challenge. Lucia also shares her designs with fans, so anyone can make their own tiny creatures!

ACTUAL SIZE!

Artist Lucia Dolgopolova

PRIZED PLAY

At a 2022 concert in Washington, D.C., U.S. musician Lizzo became the first person to play a 200-year-old crystal flute that was once owned by former U.S. President James Madison. The flute is so valuable that it was delivered to the stage by police escort.

WORLD WISH

To honor the last wish of their late father Michael Harris, his children threw his prosthetic leg into the sea off the coast of Gloucestershire, England, in the hope that it would float around the world.

REFLECTION WRITING

Italian Michele Santelia types books backward, from right to left with individual letters reversed. Using four custom blank keyboards simultaneously, he has typed more than 80 books backward in several different languages. He was inspired by the left-handed Leonardo da Vinci, who pioneered this technique of "mirror writing"—script that looks correct when reflected in a mirror.

ASPARAGUS TIPS

Jemima Packington, from Bath, England, is the world's only asparamancer. She claims to be able to predict the future by throwing asparagus spears into the air and interpreting the way in which they land.

NORTH TO SOUTH

Californian teenager Liam Garner cycled the length of the Americas from Prudhoe Bay, Alaska, to Ushuaia, Argentina, in 527 days. His 20,000-mile (32,000-km) ride took him through 14 countries. He was delayed in Colombia when a crash left him needing 40 stitches from a head wound. Before continuing on his journey, he spent a month in the hospital where he had plastic surgery to stitch his ear back together.

BARGAIN BUY

Will Sideri of Maine bought an old manuscript for $75 at an estate sale and later found out it was a 700-year-old Latin artifact worth $10,000! The parchment was part of the Beauvais Missal, a prayer book used in Catholic worship at Beauvais Cathedral in France in the late-thirteeth century.

HAM THIEF

Over a period of six years, a man who worked at a ham curing warehouse in Huelva, Spain, resold 7,000 hams that he had stolen from his employer.

DARING DRIVER

Pulled over by police officers in Chisago County, Minnesota, a man handed them his driver's license and a "Get Out of Jail Free" card from Monopoly. Sadly for him, the local sheriff's office pointed out that the state does not recognize the card as a valid document.

REUNITED AIRLINES

April Gavin's suitcase was lost during a United Airlines flight from Chicago to her home in Oregon in August 2018. Four years later, it mysteriously turned up at an airport in Houston, Texas, with its contents intact after arriving on a flight from Honduras!

300 PERCENT LARGER!

FULLY FUNCTIONAL!

SUPERSIZED SHOT

The world's largest Nerf gun measures a whopping 12.5 feet (3.81 m) long and weighs over 200 pounds (90.72 kg)! The giant version of the popular toy is fully functional and 300 percent larger than your average Nerf gun. Michael Pick created the oversized blaster in Huntsville, Alabama. He designed 12-inch (30-cm) darts that launch at 50 mph (80 kmph) with enough power to shatter glass mugs and put a hole in a watermelon!

FUNNY BONES

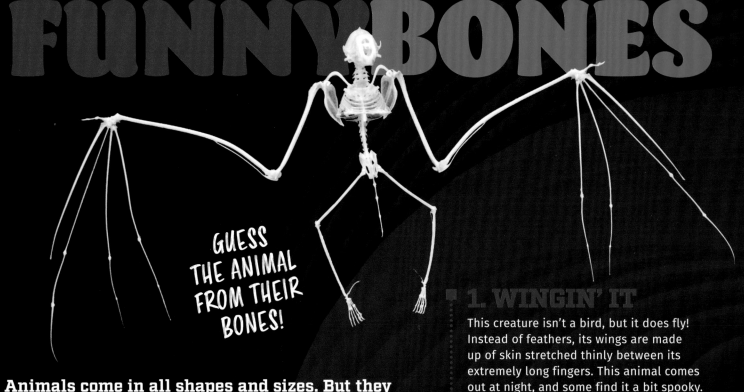

GUESS THE ANIMAL FROM THEIR BONES!

Animals come in all shapes and sizes. But they can be hard to recognize without their skin, fur, scales, or feathers! Check out these spectacular skeletons and read the clues to see if you can figure out which animal they belong to!

1. WINGIN' IT

This creature isn't a bird, but it does fly! Instead of feathers, its wings are made up of skin stretched thinly between its extremely long fingers. This animal comes out at night, and some find it a bit spooky. But these flying mammals are amazing pest control. They can eat thousands of insects in just one hour!

2. BIG BEAK

This bird's beak is about one-third of its body length! Despite its large size, the beak is very light. It helps the bird stay cool in the rainforest canopies it calls home. The beak's knife-like edges are perfect for catching small animals and cutting through yummy fruit. (And Froot Loops, if you include breakfast cereal mascots!)

3. HOME BONES

This animal has a protective shell that is part of its body. It is made up of broad, flat rib bones that are fused together. Different kinds of this animal are found on land, in fresh water, and in oceans. Some can pull their head and legs into their shell for extra protection.

4. NO BONES

Believe it or not, this animal doesn't have any bones! The skeleton you see here is actually made of cartilage. That's the same stuff that makes up the stiff, yet flexible, parts of your nose and ears! This creature's cartilage supports a pancake-shaped body used to glide above the sea floor.

BIG EYES!

5. PECULIAR PEEPERS

This bird has huge, tube-shaped eyes used for hunting prey in the dark. They can make up as much as 5 percent of the bird's body weight! These big eyes are held in place by bony rings. The rings make it impossible for the bird to move its eyes without turning its head. To make up for this, the bird is able to rotate its head almost all the way around!

IS IT A CYCLOPS?

6. LEGENDARY LOOKS

This animal's skull looks like it could belong to a one-eyed giant or cyclops. In fact, it is thought that the bones left behind by an extinct relative of this animal are what inspired the cyclops myth! What looks like an eye socket is actually where the creature's trunk would have been.

CHECK YOUR ANSWERS!

ANSWERS: 1. Bat, 2. Toucan, 3. Turtle, 4. Stingray, 5. Owl, 6. Elephant

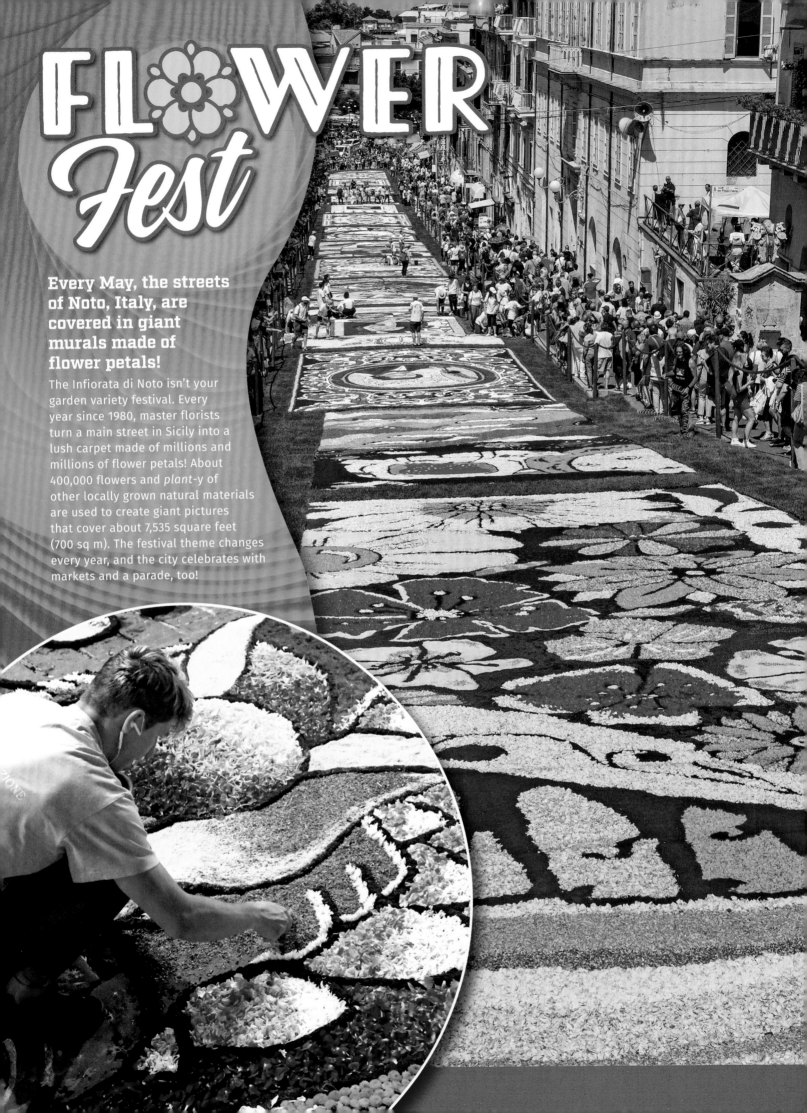

FLOWER Fest

Every May, the streets of Noto, Italy, are covered in giant murals made of flower petals!

The Infiorata di Noto isn't your garden variety festival. Every year since 1980, master florists turn a main street in Sicily into a lush carpet made of millions and millions of flower petals! About 400,000 flowers and *plant*-y of other locally grown natural materials are used to create giant pictures that cover about 7,535 square feet (700 sq m). The festival theme changes every year, and the city celebrates with markets and a parade, too!

BOULDER BUILDING

Portugal's Casa do Penedo, or Boulder House, rocks. In fact, it was built between four massive boulders during the 1970s! Everything except some furniture, doors, windows, and the roof are made from rock. Inside, there is even a sofa made of concrete that weighs almost 800 pounds (362 kg)!

CHARTING CALLS

To raise awareness of Australia's declining bird population, scientists released *Songs of Disappearance*, a CD featuring the calls of 53 of the country's most endangered birds—and it soared to number two on the national charts, ahead of the likes of Mariah Carey, Adele, and Taylor Swift. The follow-up album featured the calls of 43 of Australia's most endangered frogs.

FOREVER YOUNG

The axolotl, a salamander-like amphibian from Mexico, only fully matures into an adult if it is injected with iodine. Otherwise, it stays in juvenile form for its entire life.

STRONG STOAT

European stoats regularly hunt and kill wild rabbits, even though rabbits are five times their size.

TUNNEL RUN

The Tunnel is a 200-mile-long (322-km) ultramarathon that is run entirely inside the disused Combe Down railway tunnel near Bath, England. Racing in darkness for more than 50 hours, runners must complete 200 lengths of the tunnel, which is 1 mile (1.6 km) long.

STATE SKATE

In the summer of 2022, former Missouri State hockey player Louis Chaix inline skated 2,902 miles (4,670 km) across the U.S. He glided from Los Angeles, California, to New York City, New York, in 45 days 10 hours. He traveled through 13 states, gained 132,872 feet (40,499 m) of elevation, and skated at speeds of up to 53 mph (84 kmph).

RECLINER HIDER

Inky the cat spent three weeks on the run in a furniture factory after stowing away in a recliner chair. Randi McGlone Reyna, from Kentucky, returned her new recliner to the Big Sandy Superstore unaware that her cat was hiding inside. Inky bolted as soon as the chair was unloaded, and she hid in the store before she was finally caught.

DOUBLE TROUBLE!

TUSKED TREASURE

The Explorers Club collection in New York City has four tusks that belonged to one elephant! The extra tusks were likely caused by a genetic mutation. It's said that the elephant lived in the Congo, and the special tusks were collected after the animal's death by club member Armand Denis. Today, the natural wonder can be seen on display in the Explorers Club's Trophy Room, along with other rarities from around the world.

Pulling TEETH

Dentist Mike Foley of Tampa, Florida, put his money where his mouth is by pulling a car nearly 100 feet (30 m) with his teeth!

Dr. Mike decided it was time to show his patients just how strong a healthy set of teeth can be! Just like a superhero's cape, his customized mouthpiece transforms him into Dr. Iron Jaw and helps him conquer this feat! Ripley's sat down with the doc to grill him about his talent and learn just how powerful our chompers can be!

Q: What inspired you to perform this feat?

A: Seeing the amazing human talents in Ripley's annual books inspired me. I have every edition! It took me a while to find my unique gift, but my dental training and strong teeth became part of my "Iron Jaw" act. The circus was another inspiration. Acrobats have been known to hang by their teeth. Some pulled heavy objects using a similar mouth device like the one I designed.

DR. IRON JAW

" Please don't try this at home.

METRO MISSION
On November 16, 2022, travel blogger Lucas Wall went through all 97 Metrorail stations in Washington, D.C., in 8 hours 54 minutes.

COLLECTING CARDS
Brothers Jens Ishoy Prehn and Per Ishoy Nielsen from Denmark have a collection of more than 32,800 Pokémon cards. Their most valuable card, a first-edition Charizard, is worth about $20,000.

CAVE CONFINEMENT
Spanish extreme athlete Beatriz Flamini spent 500 days straight living in a 230-foot-deep (70-m) cave in Granada, Spain, with no human contact. During this time, she read 60 books and knitted woolly hats. When she emerged from the cave in April 2023, it was the first time she had spoken to anyone for nearly 1.5 years.

MARATHON MATES
Daniel Gallagher and Jack Meegan, both from Northern Ireland, completed the 26.2-mile (42-km) London Marathon in 2 hours 53 minutes… while handcuffed together.

MESS-FREE MERMAID
Estonian swimmer Merle Liivand (a.k.a. "Mermaid Merle") swam 31 miles (50 km) around Florida's Biscayne Bay while wearing a monofin—a swimming fin that resembles a mermaid's tail. The eco champion collected 20 pounds (9 kg) of trash from the bay during her 14-hour swim.

TRUCK TUG
Brothers-in-law John Darwen and James Baker each pulled a 1.5 ton truck around an airfield near York, England, for a distance of 32 miles (51 km) in 24 hours.

Q: Did pulling the car with your teeth hurt?

A: The appliance for my mouth spread the forces from pulling the car evenly across all my teeth. This made the task more comfortable. My neck was the most uncomfortable. I felt a lot of pressure on my neck muscles when I got the car moving.

Q: How did you prepare for the car pull?

A: Most of my preparation focused on making the device comfortable between my teeth. My first few attempts at making it were far too bulky. I settled on a simple design with a custom acrylic insert that supports my teeth and jaw.

Q: Did you practice on smaller objects?

A: Taking baby steps would make the most sense, right? I started with the goal of pulling a car. I didn't try to pull anything smaller. Now that I think about it, pulling my kids in a wagon would be a fun way to tour the neighborhood.

Q: What does it take to have teeth healthy and strong enough to pull a car?

A: It's my professional opinion, and like the old saying goes, "Please don't try this at home." It's best to leave it to the professionals, but my strong teeth are the result of brushing twice a day, flossing at least once a day, and having regular cleanings and checkups. Good genes and habits I learned from my parents help, too! Hopefully, this over-the-top performance inspires young people to take care of their teeth. Their smile can help them accomplish something incredible in the future.

Q: Are there are any other teeth-based feats of strength you hope to perform someday?

A: I'm now on the hunt to pull other vehicles! I'd love to pull an aircraft, boat, camper, or even a Zamboni! The stranger the better. I'd also like to set a distance record for pulling a car with my teeth. I'm not done exploring ways to use my teeth to do the unbelievable.

POWER PLAY
On April 5, 2023, Irish golfer Seamus Power hit back-to-back holes-in-one during the Masters Par 3 Contest at Augusta National Golf Club's course in Georgia. He aced both the eighth and ninth holes, becoming only the third player to achieve successive holes-in-one in the event's 63-year history.

BATTERY BITES
Doctors in Dublin, Ireland, removed 50 AA and AAA batteries from the abdomen of a 66-year-old woman. Five other batteries that she had swallowed had passed naturally.

SPEEDY TRIMMER
Using a trimmer, Greek barber Konstantinos Koutoupis can cut a client's hair in only 47 seconds.

FACE TUNNELS
Body piercing enthusiast James Goss has 17 flesh tunnels—rings to stretch the skin after a piercing—in his face. He had his first piercing in his lip when he was 14, and he now also has them in his nose and cheeks. He removes his septum piercing to blow his nose, and when he eats he turns his mouth piercings the opposite way to stop them from breaking.

PARK HOP
A Disney fan from Georgia visited all 12 Disney theme parks around the world and went on all 216 operating rides in 12 days. Nathan Firesheets started his three-continent, $12,000 journey in Paris, France, and finished in Florida.

CAR PARK CALENDAR
President of the Car Park Appreciation Society, Kevin Beresford spent months traveling more than 600 miles (960 km) around the UK to take photographs of parking lots. He put his favorite 12 pictures into a calendar.

Dolphin Island

A *fin*-tastic sight from above, Italy's Gallo Lungo Island is shaped like a dolphin!

From above, you can clearly make out a dolphin's nose, fins, and tail along the island's rocky coastline. Located just off the Amalfi Coast, this dolphin-shaped paradise is part of a tiny archipelago with three main islands known as Sirenusas. This region is home to several species of dolphins, making it an excellent destination for dolphin watching, too!

FLIPPIN' COOL!

PURPLE CRAB

The purple spider crab is known for its bright violet shell and spider-like body! The crab is social and peaceful, often living in small groups in Central Africa. The purple spider crab uses rotting trees as a home or builds its own in the mud of swampy areas! They measure 3 inches (7.6 cm) wide and no more than 2 inches (5 cm) tall. The crab eats dead plants and algae while burrowing and hiding in sand. The sand won't stop it from showing off its colorful shell, though!

DOWN UNDER

Beach worms up to 10 feet (3 m) long live on the eastern and southeastern coasts of Australia! They have hundreds of body segments and sharp teeth for eating dead fish or seaweed. The worms use their 0.5-inch (1.5-cm) bodies to make burrows in the sand for hiding. People often catch the beach worms to use as bait for fishing!

CATCH OF THE DAY!

BEAR JAIL

The town of Churchill in Manitoba, Canada, has a polar bear jail. Any bears that wander into town in search of food are kept in a holding facility until they can be safely released back into the wild. The jail, a former military hangar, has 28 cells that are fitted with strong metal bars and doors. Some of the cells are air-conditioned to keep the bears comfortable.

DOG RESCUE

A missing dog that fell down a large hole while walking in Derbyshire, England, was found after being sniffed out by another dog. Gracie, an eight-year-old black Labrador owned by Guy Beggs, disappeared during bad weather on a country walk. The next day, Lottie, a border collie-spaniel mix, led owner Susan Jones, who was part of the search party, to the exact hole down which Gracie had fallen.

CHEESE LABELS

Members of the Club Tyrosémiophile de France collect the artistic labels attached to round wooden boxes of Camembert cheese. One member, Serge Schéhadé from Paris, France, has over 35,000 labels, some dating back more than 100 years.

PIZZA STUNTS

Tony Gemignani, from Fremont, California, has won seven world championships as a pizza acrobat, performing tricks like tossing the dough 15 feet (4.6 m) in the air, then sliding it through his legs and around his back like a basketball.

CARD TOWER

Using no glue, Tian Rui, from Qingdao, China, built a house of playing cards 50 "stories" high. It took him just over five hours and measured 11 feet 7 inches (3.53 m) tall. He previously built a castle, based on the one from the movie *Frozen*, from 12,000 playing cards.

INFLATABLE LINE

On July 30, 2022, hundreds of people floated on swim rings at Lac Pelletier Regional Park in Wymark, Saskatchewan, Canada, to form a line that stretched 1,177 feet (359 m).

PEBBLE *Picasso*

Justin Bateman is a British artist who turns pebbles into lifelike works of art!

Justin travels the world in search of small rocks for his designs. With impeccable attention to detail, he creates images of famous people such as Abraham Lincoln and artworks like the *Mona Lisa*! Justin only uses stones he finds from the places he visits for his art. Each piece can take him hours, days, or even weeks to finish. Best of all? Justin can find inspiration and create his art wherever stones may be, from a calm beach to a noisy train station!

ONE STONE AT A TIME!

LALISA MANOBAL

MICHELANGELO'S DAVID

FRIDA KAHLO

DAVID BOWIE

GEORGE WASHINGTON

Catalog No. 16436

Tin Can Car

Retired engineer Reginald Cowper of Toronto, Canada, makes trains, boats, and cars from tin cans! This piece depicts the ultra-rare Duesenberg sports car. Cars from this brand are highly collectible—the company went defunct after making vehicles for less than 20 years!

MADE FROM RECYCLED TIRES!

Catalog No. 172584

Two-Headed Lion Tire Art

Ji Yong-Ho makes wild art out of recycled tires! Most of his work is focused on unique animals, such as this two-headed lion!

DISCOVER *Even More at a*
RIPLEY'S *Believe It or Not!*
Near You! VISIT RIPLEYS.COM

600 DIFFERENT IMAGES OF ELVIS!

Catalog No. 20935

Elvis Presley Painting

This painting has us all shook up! Artist Enrique Ramos made this eye-catching painting using 600 different images of Elvis. Despite us all knowing Elvis as a textbook tall, dark, and handsome man, he was born a natural blonde and regularly dyed his hair to its signature black.

PLUMP *my Ride*

Austrian sculptor Erwin Wurm takes sleek cars and turns them into voluptuous vehicles!

To make the sculptures in his *Fat Car* series, Erwin covers the real thing in layers of plastic and foam. After he is happy with the new size and shape, he gives it a shiny coat of paint. The result? Cars that look as soft and squishy as a marshmallow! While Erwin's creations are funny to look at, they also have a serious side. Erwin hopes they make people question the world's growing appetite to own bigger and bigger vehicles.

FEELIN' BLOATED?

TEAL ARCHES

McDonald's is famous for its golden arches. But in Sedona, Arizona, they are teal! This is because the city does not want its buildings to clash with the area's natural beauty. Teal was picked because it looks nice with the red mountains. Tourists may come for the teal arches, but they stay for the food!

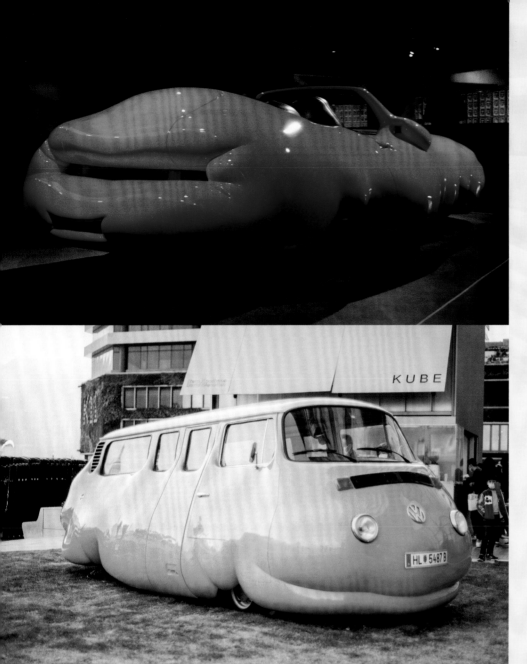

CRASH CROOKS

After two thieves stole merchandise from a clothing store in Springfield, Missouri, they made their getaways in separate cars—but crashed into each other. They then tried to flee on foot but were quickly apprehended.

VETERAN DIRECTOR

Known as the "King of Action" in his native Thailand, Chalong Pakdeevijit directed the 18-episode TV series *Skyraider* at age 91. He began his career as a cinematographer in 1950 and directed his first movie in 1968.

PRICEY PICKLE

Pickle, a work by Australian artist Matthew Griffin, consists of a ketchup-smeared pickle from a McDonald's cheeseburger stuck to the ceiling of an art gallery in Auckland, New Zealand. The artistic pickle was valued at $6,200!

POKÉ PLACE

A neighborhood in Henderson, Nevada, has streets named after famous Pokémon! There's Snorlax Lane, Jigglypuff Place, and more! So many houses were being built in the area that it was hard for construction manager Andrea Miller to come up with new street names. She got the idea to use Pokémon from her two sons. With more than one thousand Pokémon to choose from, she won't run out of names any time soon.

Later, GATOR!

TAKING A LONG, COLD NAP!

To deal with cold weather, alligators let the water freeze around their bodies—turning them into gatorcicles!

While gators wait for the ice to melt, they leave only their snouts sticking out of the ice to breathe! Frozen gators have been seen in places like North Carolina and Texas. The practice is called brumation. During the process, the reptiles' bodies slow down. In a sense, it's like they are taking a long nap!

SEA MOUSE

The sea mouse is a marine worm covered in bristles, or short hairs. The edges of the hair shine a rainbow of colors, including blues, greens, reds, and yellows! The bright colors protect it from underwater predators. The worm is about 8 inches (20 cm) long and 2 inches (5 cm) wide with a fuzzy body that looks like glass! The sea mouse hunts for crabs, squid, and other worms on the seabed 9,842.5 feet (3,000 m) deep.

OUCH! PRICKLY HAIRS!

BEACH BALLS

Round rocks known as the Moeraki Boulders rest at Koekohe Beach on the South Island in New Zealand. Some believe they are remains from a shipwreck. Others think they are alien eggs! Each sphere weighs several tons and is almost perfectly round. Visitors can see the rocks from the Moeraki Boulders Café or by walking along the shore.

SHOCK SOCK

This shocking technology gives directions! Researchers at the University of Chicago created a new form of navigation tech. Called FeetThrough, it sends a slight shock to the bottom of the foot, telling the wearer which way to go. It even improves posture by helping people feel the ground and become more aware of their surroundings. Scientists are currently working on developing FeetThrough for shoes and even socks!

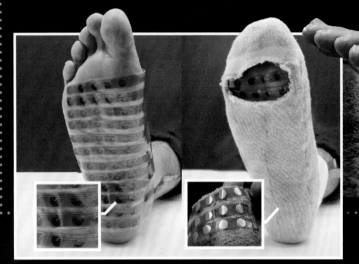

SHOCKING AND COOL!

GOAT ON WHEELS

Itty Bitty, a baby goat, learned to walk and run for the first time using a custom-made set of wheels at an animal sanctuary in Walton County, Georgia. The goat has a spinal disease that prevents her from using her back legs, so previously she could only get around by scooting on her butt.

EARTHQUAKE SURVIVOR

Alex, a husky dog, was rescued from underneath the rubble of collapsed buildings in Hatay province, Turkey, 23 days after the 2023 earthquake. He survived for over three weeks without food, water, or sunlight. He was found when rescuers heard faint cries coming from beneath a pile of fallen concrete.

HOT LOVE

A woman discovered two carpet pythons mating behind the microwave oven in the kitchen of her home in Buderim, Queensland, Australia. The snakes had slithered in through an open window. She was alerted to their presence when she saw the oven move.

BONE APPÉTIT

Dogue, a luxury café in San Francisco, caters exclusively to dogs, serving a three-course meal to its canine customers for $75.

SKYDIVING SALAMANDERS

Tiny, 4-inch-long (10-cm) wandering salamanders survive leaps of over 100 feet (30 m) from the tops of tall redwood trees in California by using the same techniques as human skydivers. They slow their descent like a parachutist, raising their chests and stretching out their limbs in a starfish pose with impressive control.

BUZZ WORD

Following the death of Queen Elizabeth II in 2022, the royal beekeeper knocked on each hive to inform the Queen's bees that the monarch had died. It is a centuries-old tradition that bees have to be told about major events in the family so that they will keep producing honey.

MUZZLE MIC

This strange-looking device is the Mutalk. It is a revolutionary Bluetooth microphone designed to keep your conversations private! Made by Shiftall, the Mutalk works like a muzzle and covers your mouth. It isolates your voice, making it hard for others to hear you and prevents ambient noise from being picked up.

PRIVACY, PLEASE!

ROBO ROVERS

Meet Agnieszka Pilat, a Polish artist who makes paintings with robot dogs!

The 60-pound (27-kg) robotic pups were built by Agility Robotics and Boston Dynamics. Named Bunny and Basia, they can collaborate with Agnieszka or even paint all on their own! To do so, they are programmed to listen to commands. Bunny and Basia can then choose how to follow these commands, like where to move their arms or how much pressure to use. They will even decide whether to make a dot or a line when they paint. The creative process is different every time, resulting in beautifully interesting pieces!

GOOD DOGGIE!

Drawn to LIFE

French artist Scaf turns empty buildings into works of art with unreal murals!

Scaf's paintings look 3D at first glance, but they are really on flat surfaces. He taught himself tricks like perspective, light, and shading to make his art jump off the walls! Scaf will often pose next to his 3D art and become part of the piece. He likes to paint in places people no longer use, like old factories or houses. Once Scaf finishes a painting, the art left behind brings the abandoned place back to life!

THIS ART REALLY JUMPS OUT!

CAVE
OF
WONDERS

Hidden deep in the jungle and mountains of Vietnam is Hang Son Doong—a cave so big a jumbo jet could fly through it!

Hang Son Doong is the largest cave in the world and millions of years old. It is more than 5.5 miles (9 km) long and some parts are more than 650 feet (200 m) tall. An entire city block, including skyscrapers, could easily fit inside the cave! Despite its great size and age, Hang Son Doong wasn't found by humans until 1990. And there is still much to discover!

Hang Son Doong has its own weather! When air from the outside world mixes with the air inside the cave, it forms dreamy clouds within the large passages.

BELOW THE SURFACE

Some cave formations inside Hang Son Doong are bigger than buildings! At 262.5 feet (80 m) tall, its Hope and Vision stalagmite—a cave formation that rises from the ground—might even be the tallest in the world.

FEELING SMALL?

There is a forest deep inside Hang Son Doong! A large hole in the ceiling lets in sunlight and makes it possible for 160-foot-tall (48.8-m) trees to grow!

No one knows where the cave's river flows. In 2019, divers followed it to an underwater tunnel that might lead to another cave. Hang Son Doong could be even bigger than we think!

There are thousands of pearls in Hang Son Doong—cave pearls, that is! They form over hundreds of years as minerals build up around grains of sand and are polished by running water.

Some of the walls in Hang Son Doong are covered in fossils! The cave formed around 2–5 million years ago, but the fossils are more than 300 million years old!

Adventure Awaits!

At the all-new Ripley's Believe It or Not! Wisconsin Dells, you can embark on a journey like no other!

Slide (really!) into a realm of curiosity and wonder! Explore winding corridors, unlock hidden chambers, discover secret passages, and stumble upon jaw-dropping artifacts from around the globe. The thrill of discovery knows no bounds! Here are just a few of the amazing artifacts you'll find at Ripley's Believe It or Not! Wisconsin Dells.

SLIDE INTO FUN!

OVER 20,000 FAKE FINGERNAILS!

Catalog No. 171392

Nail Snake

Watch your step as you explore! This python is over 8 feet (2.4 m) long and made out of more than 20,000 fake fingernails! Artist Carlos Alonso spent six months painting each one by hand. With such attention to detail, the nails look like the scales of a real snake!

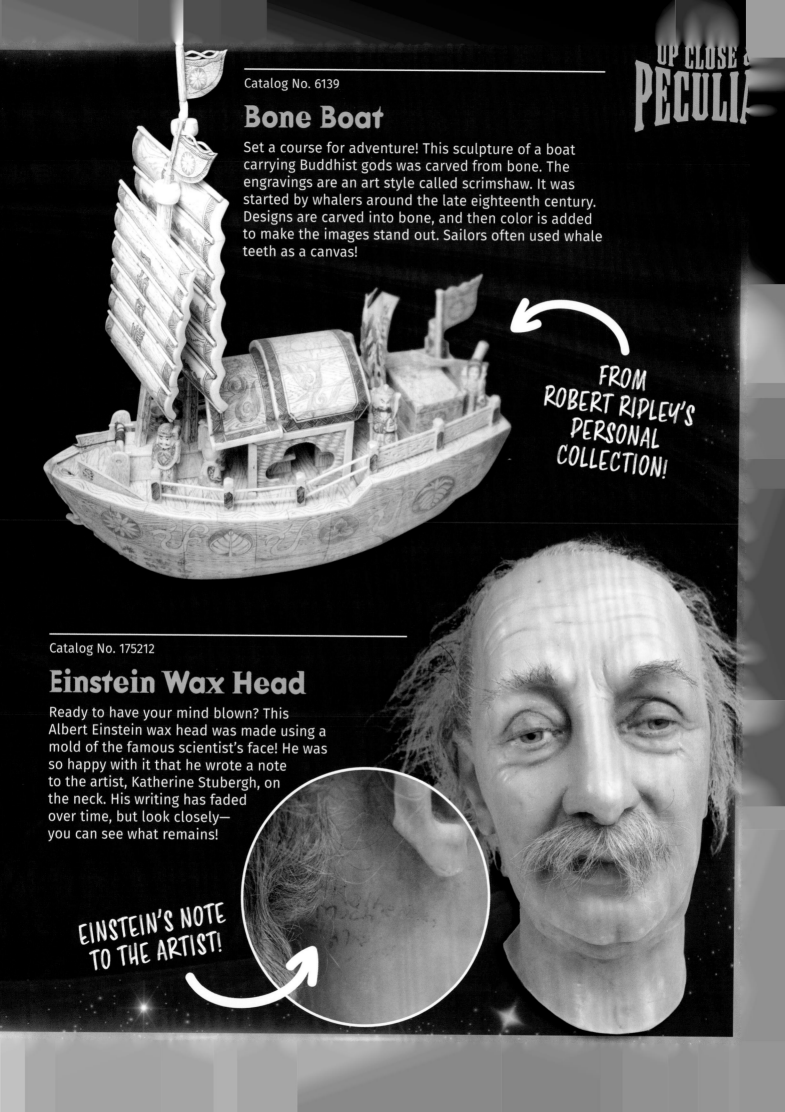

Catalog No. 6139

Bone Boat

Set a course for adventure! This sculpture of a boat carrying Buddhist gods was carved from bone. The engravings are an art style called scrimshaw. It was started by whalers around the late eighteenth century. Designs are carved into bone, and then color is added to make the images stand out. Sailors often used whale teeth as a canvas!

FROM ROBERT RIPLEY'S PERSONAL COLLECTION!

Catalog No. 175212

Einstein Wax Head

Ready to have your mind blown? This Albert Einstein wax head was made using a mold of the famous scientist's face! He was so happy with it that he wrote a note to the artist, Katherine Stubergh, on the neck. His writing has faded over time, but look closely—you can see what remains!

EINSTEIN'S NOTE TO THE ARTIST!

READY! SET! MOW!

Feeling the need for speed—uh, seed? Try the sport of lawn mower racing!

In 1973, a group of friends from West Sussex, England, set out to invent a fun and affordable sport that anyone could enjoy. A grass cutter on a cricket field caught their eye, and lawn mower racing soon became a reality! Flash forward to 2023, when the British Lawn Mower Racing Association celebrated its 50th anniversary. Fifty-two teams of drivers competed in a 12-hour, 500-lap overnight race!

TWISTED TREES

Trees can naturally fuse together, but these are the work of one man—Axel Erlandson! Some look like a cube, some form arches, and some are even woven like a basket! In 1945, Axel's family convinced him to share his hobby with the world. A year later, he opened his "Tree Circus." His twisted trees even caught the eye of Robert Ripley! Today, you can still see 25 of these amazing creations at Gilroy Gardens in California.

RIDE ON!

SPRING HAS SPRUNG

Japan's Fuji Shibazakura Festival celebrates spring's arrival with millions of pink blooms! The dreamy display is created with shibazakura, or moss phlox. They bloom in many shades of pink, white, and purple. More than 500,000 of the plants are grown in precise spots to create stunning designs. With the iconic Mt. Fuji in the background, it's no wonder the festival draws more than a half-million people each year!

PUMP IT UP

When it comes to pumpkin carving, Simon McMinnis has the mindset of go big or gourd home!

From Lancashire, England, Simon is a tiler by trade. But come spooky season, he is a pumpkin-carving master. He began carving in 2009 after growing a monster squash in his garden. Since then, he's won many awards and even sells his extremely lifelike sculptures. Simon's pumpkin portraits take him up to eight hours to make. From Boris Johnson to Slimer, there's nothing Simon can't carve! Out of the thousands of pumpkins he has carved, one of his favorite designs is a 3D sculpture of an eye.

SPOOKTACULAR SCULPTING!

SCARY REAL!

ANCIENT SMILES

A drought in the Amazon rainforest revealed ancient stone carvings of faces believed to be between 1,000 and 2,000 years old! The markings were found on a rocky edge along the river, which is to thank for their pristine preservation. Lines on the stones can even be seen where arrows and spears were sharpened!

FOREVER FACES!

HEAD-TO-HEAD

Pablo Nonato Panduro and Joel Yaicate Saavedra really put their heads together to pull off this stunt! The two acrobats known as Duo Vitalys perform feats of strength and balance. In their signature act, they balance on each other's head and have even performed it while climbing up 97 stairs!

HEADSTRONG AND TRUE!

SINGLE STREET

All 6,000 residents of Suloszowa, Poland, live on one long street!

While it isn't the only place in the world like this, the small town often goes viral online. Pictures of the village from high up reveal long, winding patches of farmland that many people find unusual or even satisfying. The locals are used to the attention, however, as the town is a popular spot for tourists. Its unique layout and scenic views even earned it the nickname "Little Tuscany."

SUPERHERO SWARM

In October 2023, the streets of Buenos Aires, Argentina, were swarmed with more than 1,000 Spider-Men! The gathering was part of an attempt to set a world record. Fans of all ages came dressed up as the web-slinging superhero (or one of his many variations from across the Spider-Verse). The result was a sea of reds, webs, and blues!

SPIDER MANIA!

NO GAS? NO PROBLEM!

The Sunswift 7 is a solar-powered car made by the University of New South Wales in Sydney, Australia. Designed to protect the environment and use energy efficiently, it went 621 miles (1,000 km) on a single charge! While the Sunswift 7 doesn't have airbags or air conditioning, and it can't drive on regular roads, it does have people talking. Hopefully, it leads to more solar cars driving through sunny countries in the future!

DUSTED DESERT

On the night of March 1, 2023, snow fell over the Sonoran Desert! Cacti were covered with up to 4 inches (10.2 cm) of snow for four hours. The strange weather happened in one of the hottest deserts in North America of all places! Snow had not fallen there in a decade. Experts called it a "once-in-a-generation" event!

SNOW WAY!

COLOSSAL FORCE

The Three Gorges Dam in China's Hubei Province moved so much water when the huge reservoir behind it was filling up in 2003 that it slowed Earth's rotation by 0.06 microseconds and shifted the poles by 0.8 inches (2 cm).

FESTIVE FOREST

In 2022, Tom Kereluk and Vince Jackman filled their home in Alberta, Canada, with 133 decorated Christmas trees. There were trees in every room, including the garage, and the largest stood 12 feet (3.6 m) tall.

LIFELONG HOME

Nancy Gifford lived in the same house in Somerset, England, for 102 years. Her family purchased it when she was two and sold it in 2023 when she was 104.

SIX STATES

Blake Hunter visited six states by bicycle in 24 hours. He started in New York and rode through Vermont, New Hampshire, Massachusetts, and Connecticut before finishing in Rhode Island, covering a distance of 141 miles (226.9 km).

MEGA MENU

In 2022, Delgadillo's Snow Cap Drive-In, an ice cream shop in Seligman, Arizona, offered 266 different milkshake flavors, including peanut butter and onion ring, banana and chili, coffee and mustard, and Oreo and fish burger.

BORROW BODS

Over 80 countries in the world have human libraries, where customers can "borrow" people instead of books. The idea behind them is to encourage people talk to those they would not normally meet.

SCARLET SEAS

Red tidal pools take shape on the coast of Heroy, Norway! The rare seaside puddle is red because of algae and bacteria that feed on salt. Don't let the beautiful shade of red fool you, though. Very few organisms can live in this salty water! These pools also give off a strong smell. This piece of nature is best seen from a distance.

Dance of the Flyers

Look to the skies! This high-flying ceremony is performed to make the gods happy and bring rain to the land!

The Danza de los Voladores, or the Dance of the Flyers, is an incredible stunt performed in Mexico and Central America. Five men in colorful clothes climb a pole that is up to 100 feet (30 m) tall to perform an ancient ceremony! Four flyers swing upside-down around the pole while the fifth plays music. The dancers do this 13 times each, making 52 spins in total, the same number of years in the Aztec calendar's century!

DANCING IN THE SKY!

10 STORIES HIGH!

REAL HUMAN HAIR!

Catalog No. 19508

Geisha Wig

Geisha don wigs, known as "katsura," during their performances. Crafted from human hair, these wigs are meticulously styled and maintained. This wig dates back to the nineteenth century!

Catalog No. 22168

Crocodile Jaw Club

This club is made from the jawbone of one of the oldest animals on the planet—a crocodile! The club is a traditional weapon used by some of the native tribes of Papua New Guinea, particularly those living along the Sepik River. The clubs are made from the lower jawbones of crocodiles, which are considered sacred animals by many of the tribes. It is highly valued among tribe members and is used for various purposes, like for protection and ceremonies!

Catalog No. 19562

Potlatch Spoon

A potlatch is an elaborate ceremony held by Indigenous people of the Pacific Northwest. During a potlatch, the host is expected to provide an extravagent feast for their guests and give away all of their earthly possessions. The carved spoon shown here was used by people of the Haida Nation to serve soups and broths. Robert Ripley acquired it in Seattle in 1936.

ONCE OWNED BY ROBERT RIPLEY

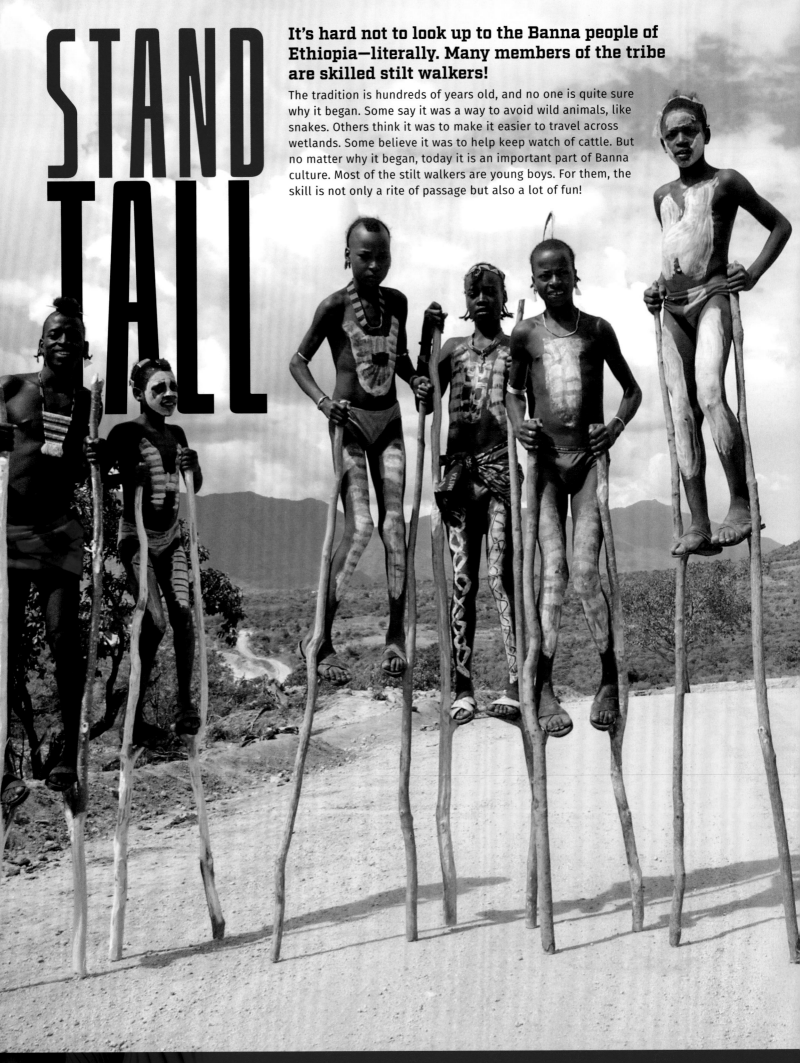

STAND TALL

It's hard not to look up to the Banna people of Ethiopia—literally. Many members of the tribe are skilled stilt walkers!

The tradition is hundreds of years old, and no one is quite sure why it began. Some say it was a way to avoid wild animals, like snakes. Others think it was to make it easier to travel across wetlands. Some believe it was to help keep watch of cattle. But no matter why it began, today it is an important part of Banna culture. Most of the stilt walkers are young boys. For them, the skill is not only a rite of passage but also a lot of fun!

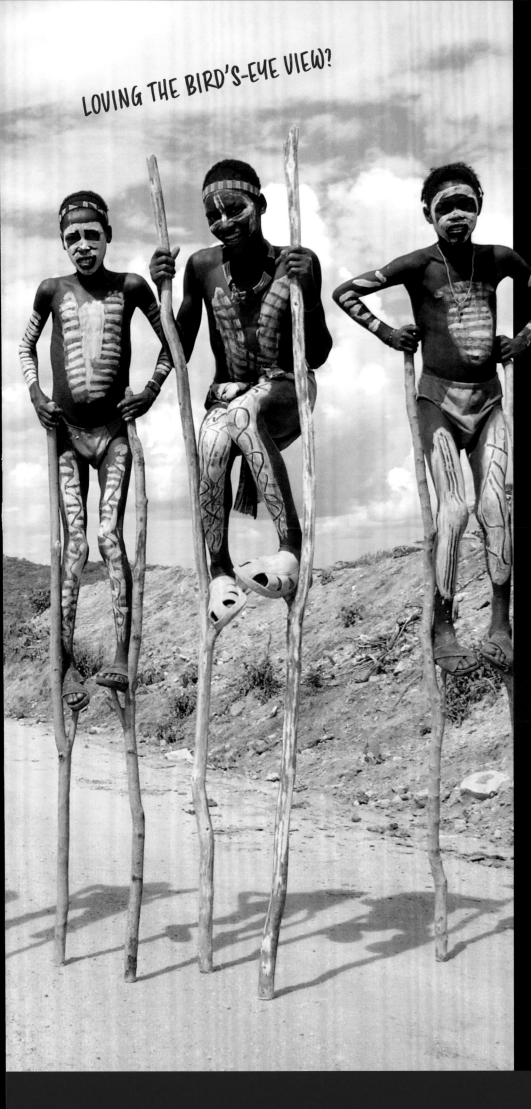

LOVING THE BIRD'S-EYE VIEW?

CADAQUÉS CHEERS
The Spanish town of Cadaqués has a replica of the Statue of Liberty, but with both hands raised as though she is cheering, as well as a torch in each hand.

FORGER HONORED
English-born Francis Greenway, a convicted nineteenth-century forger, appeared on the first Australian $10 bill printed in 1966—and remained on it for 27 years until 1993.

CONVERTED JAIL
A Margaritas Mexican restaurant in Concord, New Hampshire, is located in an old jail. The police building closed in 1975, but Margaritas placed tables inside of the cells and converted it into a restaurant. The building is said to be haunted by a spirit named George.

MASS MOVE
Rio de Janeiro in Brazil was the capital of Portugal from 1808 to 1821 after the Portuguese royal family fled there to escape from Napoleon Bonaparte's invading French forces. The Portuguese royal family, its court, and senior officials—totaling nearly 10,000 people—transferred from Lisbon to the then-Portuguese colony of Brazil.

LONG LIVES
The Museum of Longevity in Lerik, Azerbaijan, contains tributes to hundreds of centenarians in a region where life expectancy is much higher than average. At one time, one percent of Lerik's residents were over 100 years old.

SAFETY NET
When building San Francisco's Golden Gate Bridge, Joseph Strauss, the chief structural engineer, insisted on the installation of a safety net even though it would cost $130,000. During the four years of the bridge's construction (1933–37), the net saved the lives of 19 men—who later named themselves the "Halfway to Hell Club."

FRAGRANT FUEL
Japan's small scenic Amaterasu Railway runs on a biodiesel made from leftover oil and ramen noodle broth. The broth is supplied by local restaurants, and the train leaves a delicious smell as the fuel burns.

WALK IT OUT

The sea robin is a type of fish, but it can fly like a bird, walk like a mammal, and croak like a frog! Kind of. The colorful creature glides above the ocean floor with wide fins that stick out from its body like the wings of an airplane. In front of those wings are a set of leg-like spines the fish uses to pull itself across the sand and feel for food. The spines are actually part of the sea robin's fins that have evolved to sense prey hiding in the sand. As for the croaking? The fish can make sounds by using a special muscle to hit its swim bladder.

FISH LEGS!

BLOW UP

This camel isn't sticking its tongue out—it's showing off for the ladies! The one-humped, or dromedary, camel has a unique organ called a "dulla" in its throat. To make the dulla come out of its mouth, the camel fills the sac up with air like a balloon! It is mostly male camels that do this. They make a gurgling sound with the dulla to get the attention of female camels and let other males know to stay away!

HORNEDSCREAMER

The horned screamer bird of South America grows a long, unicorn-like spine out of its forehead!

The horn is unlike anything else seen in the bird world. It is made of cartilage, like your nose and ears, and can grow up to 6 inches (15.2 cm) long! Bird experts believe the strange spine is just for looks. It is barely attached to the horned screamer's skull and breaks off when it gets too long. (Don't worry, it grows back.) So it is not much help in a fight—but that doesn't mean the bird can't defend itself! Each wing has a sharp bone spur used in battles for mates.

LOOKING FLY

Birds might not have hair, but that doesn't stop them from sporting stylish—and not-so-stylish—'dos! If you need ideas for your next trip to the hair salon, look no further than this list of bizarre feather fashions.

BOWL CUT

The Gloster canary is a small bird with a big look. The canary has flat feathers on its head that resemble hair trimmed into a bowl cut! Gloster canaries are not found in the wild. They were first bred in England in 1925 by crossing together multiple kinds of canaries. That's how they got their stylish look! They are also famous for their beautiful singing, which is just right for a bird with a Beatles haircut!

NICE 'DO!

NOW THAT'S UNUSUAL!

BALDING BIRD

The Budapest short-faced tumbler isn't your typical pigeon. For one, the bird is bald around its eyes! Not only that, but with eyes that bulge out, a teeny beak, and a pointy head, it looks like it's straight out of a cartoon. It was bred in the late nineteenth century by two brothers in Budapest hoping to make a bird that could fly super far. This special pigeon could soar for five whole hours! But even with its amazing flying skills, its silly appearance is what got everyone talking. It's a bird no one can forget!

MARVELOUS MULLET

Is it just us or does this bird look like Elvis? The umbrellabird lives in the rainforests of Central and South America. The bird is known for its unique appearance. The males have an umbrella-like crest on their heads. Almost like a mullet! The birds even have an inflatable pouch! It hangs from their throats and can grow more than 13 inches (33 cm) long! The male umbrellabird will inflate their pouches during mating season.

WATTLE IS THAT?

CROWN OF FEATHERS

This bird is fly! The royal flycatcher is an unsuspecting beauty of a bird. It's found in the tropical regions of Central and South America. The royal flycatcher has a vibrant crest on its head. The crest is rarely seen and isn't always on display. The royal flycatcher uses its crest for mating and displays of dominance. Hidden on the head of the bird, the crest puffs up and gives the bird an eye-catching look. Talk about a hairstyle!

FEELING FANCY

Want to look distinguished? Try a mustache! It seems to work for the male three-wattled bellbird, at least. This Central American bird has three long, black flaps of skin called wattles around its beak. Besides its fabulous facial flaps, the three-wattled bellbird is also known for its loud call. The sound can be heard from more than 0.5 mile (0.8 km) away!

BEARDED BEAUTY

This bizarre bird has a... beard? Tūī are extravagant birds that live in New Zealand. They're found on the main islands. Tūī are known for their lovely singing. You might hear their songs first before you see them. You can spot them by their distinguished white feathers under their throat that resemble a beard. Tūī are important birds because they help to spread pollen from flower to flower.

SINKING FEELING

In the coastal jungles of Mexico, there's a swimming hole with a secret—an underwater river that even has its own island!

The bizarre body of water is part of Cenote Angelita. A cenote is a sinkhole that is always filled with water. From above, Cenote Angelita seems like a regular pond. But dive down about 100 feet (30 m) and you'll find a swirling river of fog. It is filled with large tree branches, and a small hill peeks above its surface. The fog is actually a 10-foot-thick (3-m) cloud of toxic gas that floats between two layers of water: fresh water above and seawater below. When these layers mix with hydrogen sulfate, that is what causes the underwater river effect!

SUPER SURGERY

In 2022, military surgeon Andrii Verba miraculously removed a live, unexploded grenade from the chest of a Ukrainian soldier—without setting it off. Due to the risk of explosion, two military engineers were on hand throughout and disposed of the grenade after it was removed.

FOOD ORDER

When six-year-old Mason Stonehouse, from Chesterfield Township, Michigan, borrowed his dad Keith's cell phone to play a game, he opened the Grubhub app and ordered nearly $1,000 worth of food, including jumbo shrimp and pizza, from several restaurants.

GOLDMINE JEANS

A pair of 1880's Levi's jeans that were found in an abandoned mine sold at auction in Aztec, New Mexico, in 2022 for $87,400. Amazingly, the jeans were still in wearable condition.

POTTERY MOUNTAIN

Monte Testaccio, an artificial mound in Rome, Italy, is made up of 53 million pieces of broken pottery. Composed of pottery fragments discarded during the Roman Empire, it is nearly 2,000 years old, stands 115 feet (35 m) high, and covers an area of 215,278 square feet (20,000 sq m).

TWO TEETH

A man from Dongguan, China, was shocked to find two human teeth embedded in his face six days after accidentally colliding with another player during a basketball game. He only decided to go to the hospital when the wound above his eye began to emit a foul smell.

CHICKEN ASSAULT

In 2023, a 36-year-old woman from Eagle Lake, Minnesota, was charged with hitting her boyfriend on the back of the head with a whole chicken.

CAP LANDSCAPES

Artist Mito Nishikura, from Osaka, Japan, paints tiny, detailed landscapes onto recycled plastic bottle caps. Although each cap measures just 1.2 inches (3 cm) in diameter, she paints using only a very fine paintbrush—and without a magnifying glass. It takes her three hours to finish each cap artwork.

FRESH WATER

SALT WATER

ROOTS OUT

The Tree of Life on the Washington State coast stretches between two cliffs! Wind and waves have washed away the ground below the spruce tree for years, leaving its roots almost completely exposed. Yet the tree hangs on against all odds and keeps growing healthy green leaves. Experts agree that the tree will eventually fall, but no one knows when. For now, the Tree of Life remains a symbol of strength for many.

ALL GEARED UP!

Catalog No. 170020

Bicycle Parts Dog

Artist Nirit Levav Packer creates lifelike sculptures of dogs out of discarded bicycle parts! She scours garbage bins, garage sales, and bike shops throughout Tel Aviv for parts, then welds them together to create various breeds of dogs. This sculpture of a majestic saluki is made entirely of gears.

ANIMALS WITH FIVE LEGS ARE KNOWN AS PENTAPEDS!

Catalog No. 170033

Bottle Cap Flamingo

Molly B. Right of Charleston, South Carolina, collects vintage soda bottle caps and uses them to create elaborate mosaic portraits! This Caribbean pink flamingo is made from over 2,000 bottle tops and weighs more than 30 pounds (13.6 kg). She often spends months collecting caps of just the right color to fulfill her artistic vision!

MORE THAN 2,000 BOTTLE CAPS!

Catalog No. 172330

Five-Legged Alligator

Discovered in North Florida, this alligator boasts a fully developed fifth leg protruding from its side! Animals with five legs, known as pentapeds, are very rare. Kangaroos are the sole example of an animal that uses their tail enough while moving around for it to be considered a fifth "leg!"

EXTRA LEG!

SCONE FAN

Over a period of 10 years, Sarah Merker from London, England, ate a baked scone at all 244 National Trust locations in the UK and ranked every one according to quality on her blog.

LONG SHOT

Jeremy Ware sank a backward basketball shot from a distance of 85.5 feet (26 m)—about the length of two buses—in San Antonio, Texas.

KITE CONTEST

Before beginning construction work on the Niagara Falls Suspension Bridge in 1848, engineers organized a kite-flying contest to secure a line across the gaping gorge. A 16-year-old local boy, Homan Walsh, won the $5 prize by being the first to fly his kite the 800-foot (244-m) distance across the river from the Canadian side so that its string could be tied to a tree on the U.S. side.

RADIO HOST

Mary McCoy has spent over 72 years as a radio presenter. At just 12 years old, she worked five days a week as a radio host for KMCO Radio in Huntsville, Texas. In 2023, she was still presenting her two-hour *Best In Country Classics* show six days a week on the same station, now called K-STAR. As a young singer in 1955, she once shared a stage with the up-and-coming Elvis Presley.

CONCRETE *Jungle*

Imagine sleeping high up in the trees, but with all the comforts of a modern hotel!

That's what it's like at Sanya Beauty Crown Hotel on China's Hainan Island. It has nine buildings shaped like trees with branches, trunks, and leaves! Some say they look like LEGO pieces, but it's at night when the hotel really shines—literally. When it gets dark, the whole place lights up in different colors and looks like a magical forest!

RAINBOW RESIDENCE

On a street of mostly tans and grays, Carabanchel 24 can't be missed! The colorful apartment building can be found in Madrid, Spain. Its rainbow walls are the work of architect Rafael Cañizares Torquemada. He was inspired by Swiss-German painter Paul Klee. He used similar blocks of color in his art during the early 1900s. Built between 2007 and 2010, Carabanchel 24's patchwork paint job has more than a dozen different hues!

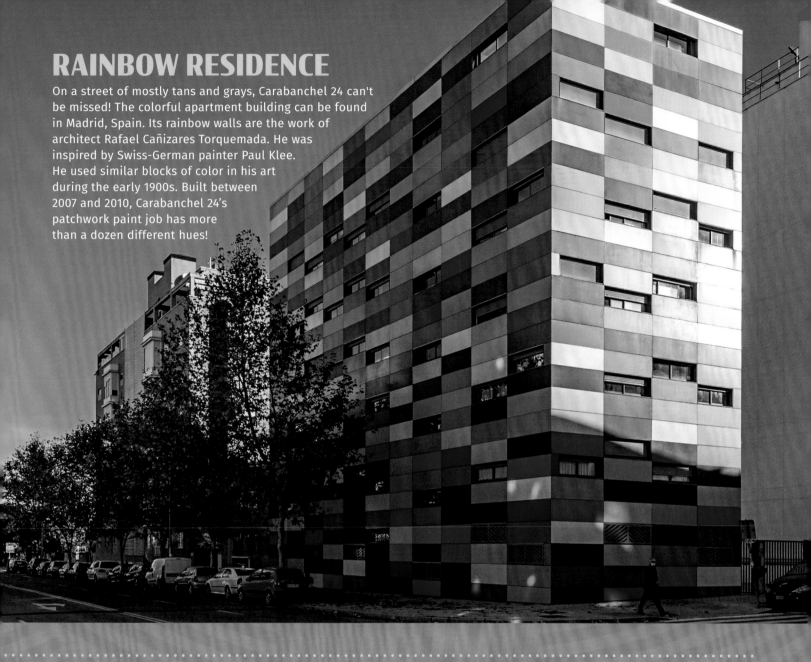

LEGO BRIDGE?

COLORFUL CROSSING

This bridge in Wuppertal, Germany, looks like it's made from giant LEGO bricks! But don't worry, it's not really plastic. In 2011, the city asked street artist Megx to transform a plain, gray bridge into something fun. Inspired by his daughters' love of the colorful toy blocks, Megx and his team spent almost two weeks painting the bridge. The change was a huge hit! People love the brick bridge so much that the city brought Megx back to paint another one in 2020.

SEED SKYDIVING

Luigi Cani dove into saving the environment... no, literally! He jumped out of a plane and planted 100 million trees in the Amazon rainforest!

The Brazilian man is known for his extreme skydiving stunts, but this jump was extra special. While falling, Luigi opened a huge box filled with seeds from 27 kinds of trees, scattering them over the rainforest. The stunt took Luigi five years to plan. He even made sure to use seeds from plants native to that area of the rainforest! The trees growing from the seeds are being monitored by satellites. Next, Luigi hopes to do something that will help clean up the plastic in the ocean. Knowing Luigi, it's sure to be incredible!

SEEDS FROM THE SKY!

ONE IN A MELON

Most people throw coins in a fountain and make a wish. In Moscow, Russia, watermelons fill the fountain at the famous GUM shopping mall! The fruity fountain holds 5 tons of watermelons during the summer. You can buy a whole melon or enjoy a cup of melon slices and fruit juices. The delicious display is just one of the unique ways the mall marks the changing of the seasons during the year.

CALCULATOR MUSIC

South Korean artist Chaco Chaco plays popular songs, including works by Daft Punk, on up to five pocket musical calculators at a time. He uses AR7778 calculators, which make music when their Time/Date buttons are pressed twice.

SAVED MANUSCRIPT

In 1940, German-born American author H. A. Rey and his wife escaped from Paris, France, on bicycles built out of spare parts just hours before the city fell to the Nazis. Among the few possessions that the couple managed to take with them was the illustrated manuscript for his then-unpublished book, *Curious George*.

BEARD CHAIN

Facial hair enthusiasts at a bar in Casper, Wyoming, stood side by side and clipped their beards together to create a beard chain that measured 150 feet (46 m) long.

SONIC COLLECTION

Barry Evans, of Dayton, Texas, has 3,050 items of Sonic the Hedgehog memorabilia, which he collected over the course of 30 years. It includes giant statues of Sonic and his sidekick Tails that were once decorations at a Toys"R"Us store.

WRONG MESSAGE

American author Peter Benchley regretted writing his best-selling novel *Jaws*, where a community is terrorized by a man-eating great white shark, because it made people too afraid of sharks and helped push some shark species toward extinction. So he spent the remainder of his life as an activist for shark conservation.

STEER CLEAR!

Ever seen a bull riding shotgun? In Nebraska, a steer named Howdy Doody does just that! He loves riding beside his owner, Lee Meyer, in a big Ford sedan modified to fit the black bovine. Howdy Doody is more than just livestock to Lee. He even knows commands like "come here" and "back up!" Locals know him well and often see him riding in parades. However, the police once gave Lee a warning for driving through town with his bull buddy—it seems having Howdy Doody in the car can be quite the safety hazard!

WONDER WORM

Nine-year-old Barnaby Domigan found a gigantic 3-foot-long (0.9-m) earthworm in the backyard of his parents' house in Christchurch, New Zealand.

POLICE SQUIRRELS

Police officers in Chongqing, China, have trained six squirrels to sniff out drugs. With their keen sense of smell, squirrels are not only skilled detectors but being smaller and faster, they can reach high and awkward spots that are inaccessible to sniffer dogs.

PERFUME POUCH

The male greater sac-winged bat of Central and South America attracts a female by sucking up a few drops of his urine and transferring it into the special pouches on his wings. The scent of his urine, mixed with a secretion from a gland on his chest, apparently proves irresistible.

NO VOMIT

Mice are unable to vomit. They have fewer diaphragm muscles than most other mammals and lack the brain signal to throw up.

MIRACLE CAT

Carol Swanson's black and white American shorthair cat, Sox, miraculously survived a fall of nearly 100 feet (30 m) from her seventh-floor apartment in Leeds, England.

TWO-WAY HOLE

Jellyfish have just one hole on their body for doing two very important things—eating *and* pooping. The jellyfish uses its tentacles to push prey into its mouth, where it is digested and the goodness is absorbed. Then the poop is pushed back out through the same hole.

DINO *Bird*

Birds are some of the closest living relatives to dinosaurs, and the hoatzin makes that pretty clear!

The hoatzin resembles a late Jurassic-era dinosaur. Hoatzin chicks even have claws on their wings to climb back into their nests! What's even weirder is that they have a digestive system similar to a cow. The hoatzin only eats vegetation, which gets fermented in its stomach. Smelly vapors exhaled by the bird give it the nickname "stinkbird."

BIRD OR DINOSAUR?

BABY WITH CLAWS!

Queen's Head
rock formation

ROCKING OUR WORLD!

HOODOO STONES

Rocks from the Yehliu Geopark in Taiwan look like they come from another planet! Known as hoodoo stones, these curious rocks have funky shapes and sizes. Some are like mushrooms and candles, but the most famous is the "Queen's Head." It's said to have once resembled England's Queen Elizabeth I. The hoodoo stones continue to change their unique shapes due to weather, sea erosion, and people touching them.

PORTUGAL'S PORTAL

In Portugal, there is a lake with a hole that is actually a tunnel! It's known as Covão dos Conchos and found in the Serra da Estrela mountains. Built in 1955 for a hydroelectric project, the tunnel connects two lakes, and the water hole provides fresh water to nearby towns. Since the mountain lake's tunnel is man-made, people think it looks like a sci-fi portal!

ANOTHER DIMENSION?

RIPLEY'S EXCLUSIVE

Extreme PUTTING

Ben Fjeld turns boredom into stardom with his unbelievable trick shots!

Ripley's put the TikToker's creativity to the test at Ripley's Crazy Golf in Myrtle Beach, South Carolina! Surrounded by inspiration, like 360-degree loops, billiards-style putting, and even zip-lining, Ben created a crazy course of his own and made one of his most challenging trick shots yet!

Q: When did you first discover your talent for trick shots?

A: I've been interested in trick shots since I was about 10, inspired by Dude Perfect. I started making videos of basketball trick shots and was even featured in a talent show video in fifth grade with friends.

Q: What's your secret to staying motivated through long projects?

A: I have a natural determination and patience that keeps me going, even if a trick shot requires multiple adjustments or takes hours. I could work for 12 hours straight, aside from bathroom breaks. The process is a roller coaster of emotions, from initial excitement to frustration, then to a mix of denial and laughter.

Q: Can you describe one of your most challenging trick shots?

A: One of my most challenging shots was a ping pong trick shot that took nine hours and involved complex bounces and ramps. However, the luckiest and most challenging was a world record shot, where I threw a CD into a game console from 36 feet (11 m) away in just six attempts!

Q: Has visiting places like Ripley's Crazy Golf inspired you in any way?

A: Absolutely. Unique features like loop-de-loops and the zip line at Ripley's have given me ideas for new trick shots. I'm even considering using a zip line at a local park for a future shot!

LIGHTEN UP

Most flowers are only enjoyed in the light, but the firefly petunia glows in the dark! This new plant was made by scientists at the Light Bio company. They used genes from a glowing mushroom to give the firefly petunia its special shine. Light Bio began selling the plant in 2024. It does not need any special food or conditions to glow, so even people without green thumbs can have a glowing, green house plant!

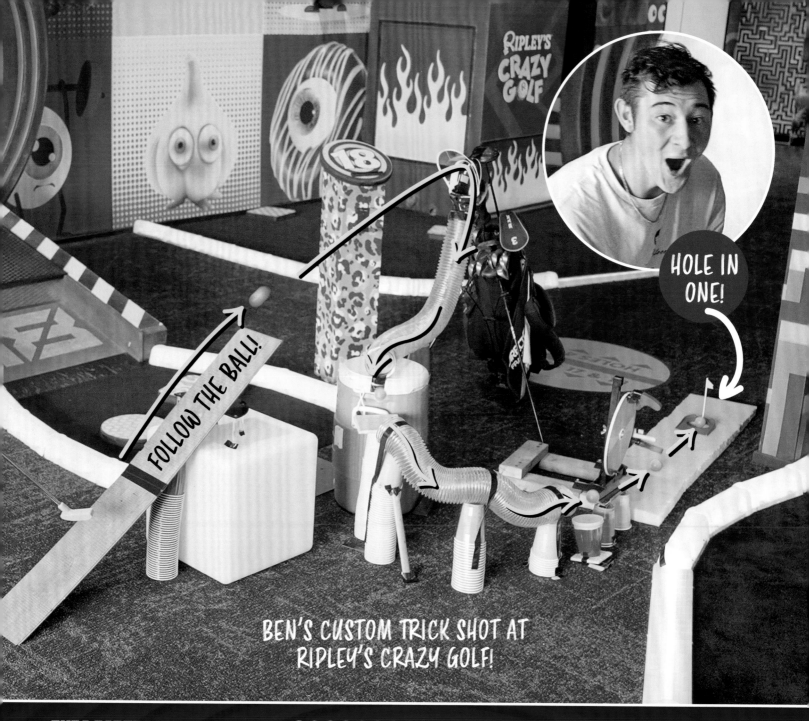

RIPLEY'S CRAZY GOLF

HOLE IN ONE!

FOLLOW THE BALL!

BEN'S CUSTOM TRICK SHOT AT RIPLEY'S CRAZY GOLF!

PYRO PORTRAITS
Nigerian artist Alex Peter Idoko creates amazingly lifelike portraits with fire, razor blades, and sandpaper. He has perfected the art of pyrography, where he uses carefully controlled gas-powered torches and hot pokers to burn scorch marks into a wooden canvas. With razor blades and sandpaper, he then lightens the shades of the burned areas to create the final image.

MEAT FEAST
Des Breakey ate 124 kebabs in December 2022, traveling to different kebab shops in Manchester, England, every day. He consumed a total of 250,000 calories and even his Christmas dinner was a kebab.

SHORT BORDER
The border between the English counties of Northamptonshire and Lincolnshire is only 62 feet (19 m) long.

Wrong Way
New York City I, an artwork by Dutch abstract painter Piet Mondrian, has been accidentally hanging upside down in various galleries around the world for over 75 years. This adhesive-tape version of his oil painting *New York City* was first displayed in 1945, but the mistake was not discovered until 2022.

SWEATY SMELL
Brazilian model Wanessa Moura launched a new perfume, "Fresh Goddess," which included her body sweat as an ingredient. Each bottle contains 0.27 ounces (8 ml) of her perspiration.

SPY CODE
The first spy to use "007" as a code was John Dee, who served Queen Elizabeth I of England in the sixteenth century—four centuries before the James Bond books and films.

NICE DICE
Oklahoma City-based artist Steven Paul Judd created a portrait of nineteenth-century Native American leader Sitting Bull out of 20,068 dice.

NEW NAME
For more than 30 years, film directors who wanted to disown a movie they had worked on used the pseudonym "Alan Smithee" instead of their own name.

OUTSIDE the BOX

French artist Olivier Grossetête took box forts to the next level when he used more than 1,500 pieces of cardboard to create a 45-foot-tall (13.7-m) building!

No machines were used to build the cardboard creation. Instead, Olivier was helped by hundreds of volunteers—even kids! The tower was made for the 2023 NOVUM Summer Festival in Newcastle, England. At the end of the two-day event, Olivier let people tear the art piece down! They pulled, pushed, jumped, and stomped until it was flat. It was Olivier's out-of-the-box way of bringing people together.

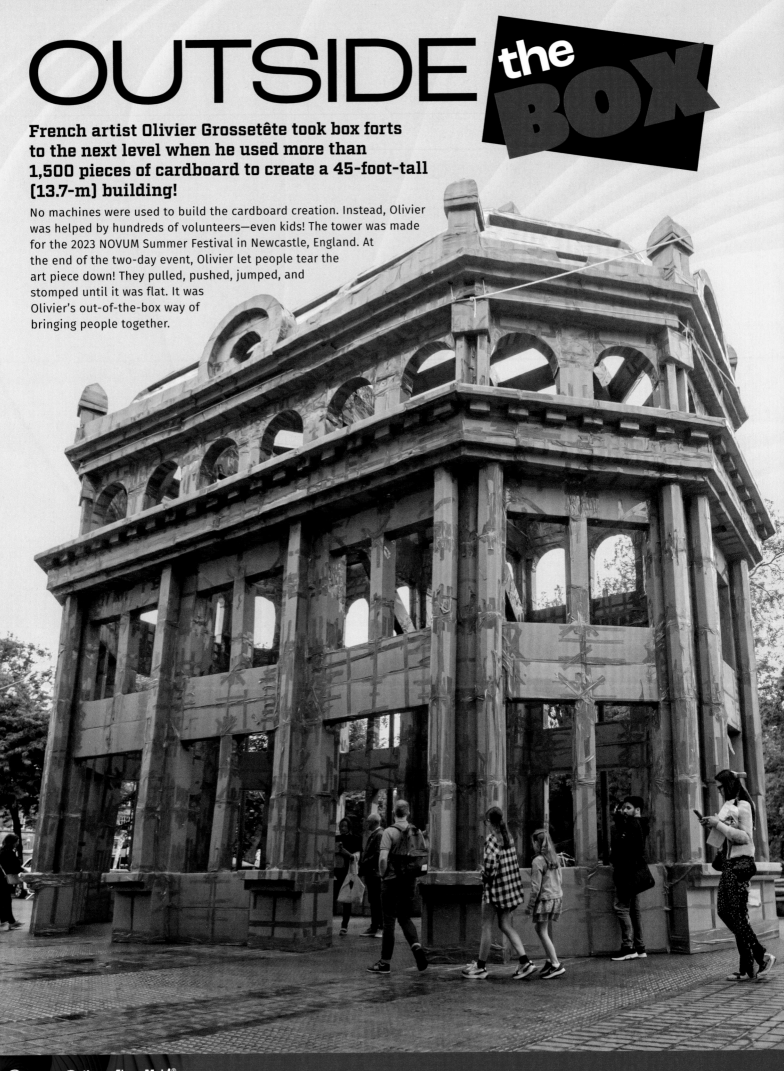

BUILT COMPLETELY BY HAND!

FUN TO KNOCK DOWN!

LIMP LOVE

For four years, limping was fashionable in nineteenth-century England. This was because the Prince of Wales's wife, Alexandra of Denmark, walked with a limp after an illness in 1867 and other society ladies wanted to copy her. To cater to the demand for the "Alexandra Limp," an Edinburgh shoemaker sold shoes with one high and one low heel.

METAL MARRIAGE

At their wedding in Idaho Falls in 2022, heavy metal music fans Madi Danger and her groom Jay Aspen exchanged electric guitars instead of rings. They walked down the aisle to the sound of Ozzy Osbourne and left for the reception in a black hearse. They had a black wedding cake decorated with red roses, which they cut with an ornate dagger.

NEW NAMES

The chess piece known as the "bishop" in English is called the "jester" in France, the "runner" in Germany, and the "elephant" in Russia.

BAD BATHROOM

British travel blogger Graham Askey visited 91 countries and spent $165,000 in search of... the world's worst bathroom. He found it in Ayni, Tajikistan—a 5-foot-tall (1.5-m) wooden stall that was infested with rats and venomous snakes and did not have toilet paper.

WEE OR WINE

Wine lactone, the pleasant-smelling compound found in many wines, was first discovered in koala urine.

BIG LOSS

Over-confident Dorset soccer fan and businessman Karl Baxter was left with 18,000 unwanted T-shirts that wrongly proclaimed England as winners of the 2022 World Cup. He had them printed ahead of the quarter-final game against France, which England lost 2-1.

KEY CALAMITY

Renée Lariviere from Ontario, Canada, was rushed to the hospital after a bizarre accident left her with a car key stuck in her face. A friend had casually tossed Renée the key, but it bounced off her hand, punctured her cheek, and wedged 1.5 inches (3.75 cm) deep into her nasal cavity. A surgeon was able to remove the key and stitch up the wound.

TWIN TORTOISE

In September 2022, Janus, a two-headed Greek tortoise at the Geneva Natural History Museum in Switzerland, turned 25 years old!

The tortoise would not have survived long in the wild because he is unable to retract his heads into his shell to hide from predators. As well as two heads, he has two hearts, two pairs of lungs, and two distinct personalities. The right head is more adventurous, while the left head is quieter but loves to eat. For exercise, Janus is taken on regular walks and also rides on a custom-made skateboard.

TIGER TERROR

Archana Choudhary fought a tiger with her bare hands for two minutes to save her 15-month-old son after the beast attacked him in Madhya Pradesh, India. The tiger sank its teeth into the boy's head and started dragging him into the jungle. But Archana hit back and her screams alerted villagers who chased the tiger away.

ENGINE EXCURSION

A four-month-old shih tzu–Pomeranian mix named BonBon survived a 30-mile (48-km) ride in a car's engine compartment. She secretly climbed in, riding all the way to Kansas City, Missouri, and was only discovered when someone heard whimpering coming from a parked car. BonBon was later reunited with her grateful owner, Thatiana Chavez.

SNOWMAN STATUE

In April, villagers in New Glarus, Wisconsin, burn a giant snowman effigy called the Böögg to banish winter. The 5-foot-tall (1.5-m) snowman is filled with hay and his head is stuffed with fireworks. The ritual is based on a larger event in Switzerland in recognition that the village was founded by Swiss settlers and still has a large Swiss community.

PRESIDENTIAL PETS

The White House is no stranger to odd pets. They're about as American as apple pie! Check out the weird presidential pets that have walked through the halls of history.

GOT MILK?

President William Howard Taft had a cow, Pauline Wayne, who gave his family fresh milk and butter. Her nickname was Queen of the Capital Cows, and she weighed 1,500 pounds (680 kg) at four years old! Fans of Pauline could buy her milk in souvenir bottles for 50 cents each.

ONE-LEGGED ROOSTER!

REBECCA RACCOON!

President Calvin Coolidge had a pet raccoon named Rebecca! She was known for causing chaos for the White House Staff. From breaking free of cages to tearing up clothes, Rebecca kept the President on his toes! She was given a wooden house outside near the President's office.

President Theodore Roosevelt and his family owned a one-legged rooster named Fierce! Roosevelt had many animals for pets with personalities as big as his. Fierce was strong enough to stand on one leg! How cool is that?

President Herbert Hoover adopted an opossum found on the South Lawn of the White House! He named him Billy Possum, who used Rebecca the Raccoon's cage as its home.

Catalog No. 175663

White House Gavel

This gavel is more than just a striking, wooden hammer—it's a genuine piece of U.S. history! It boasts a unique connection to the nation's capital. The gavel was crafted from wood salvaged during the White House renovation led by President Truman in 1950!

Catalog No. 175638

Zappas
Bronze Medal

The Zappas Olympics were a series of athletic events held in Athens, Greece, in the 1800s. Although not an international event, the Zappas Olympics were significant to the Olympic Games of today. The modern arrangement of gold, silver, and bronze medals serving as awards for first, second, and third prizes was established according to the original plan of the Zappas Olympics!

PRIZE OF THE ZAPPAS OLYMPICS!

Catalog No. 175637

1968 Grenoble Winter Olympics Torch

The 1968 Winter Olympics Torch traveled over 4,487 miles (7,222 km) to get from Olympia, Greece, to the Games in Grenoble, France! About half of the distance was covered on foot, while the other half was traversed by ski, horseback, bicycle, car, and even rowboat!

Catalog No. 174767

Theodore Roosevelt Top Hat

This hat was once owned by President Theodore Roosevelt! It has its own silk-lined box, and the inside of the hat is stamped with the president's name.

Dizzying DIAMOND

Above Dashbashi Canyon, in southern Georgia, is a glass bridge stretching 787 feet (240 m) long!

If you dare to cross, in the middle is a diamond-shaped bar dangling above the ground. It is said to be one of the largest- and highest-hanging structures in the world! From there, panoramic views of nature, from waterfalls to caves, can be seen.

DON'T LOOK DOWN!

ZIP-LINING ON A BIKE!

SOLE SURVIVOR

Serbian flight attendant Vesna Vulović miraculously survived falling more than 33,000 feet (10,000 m) when her airplane crashed in January 1972 in the modern-day Czech Republic while en route from Stockholm in Sweden to Belgrade. While all of the other 27 crew and passengers were sucked out of the plane when the cabin depressurized, Vulović survived because she was trapped by a food cart in the tail end of the fuselage. Although she suffered a fractured skull, two broken legs, three broken vertebrae, and several broken ribs, she was eventually able to walk again.

FLAG FEAT

Sixteen-year-old Hassan Dawy from Lebanon can identify all of the world's national flags in four minutes—it took him over 1,000 attempts to be so quick. He has loved geography since he was very young.

WALKING CURE

Swiss-born American tennis player Richard Norris Williams was advised to have his legs amputated when they became severely frostbitten after he spent several hours in freezing water following the sinking of the RMS *Titanic* in April 1912. But instead he walked off the pain and within two months he was playing again. In August 1912, he won the mixed doubles with Mary Browne at the U.S. National Championships.

TRASH BINS

Alexander Smoljanovic has a collection of more than 100 full-size wheelie trash bins in the garden of his home in Germany. His passion for them started 15 years ago and he has examples from the U.S., Australia, the UK, France, and Germany in a wide range of colors. He also has over 300 mini wheelie bins.

YIKES!

CHILD EATER

Standing tall in the center of Bern, Switzerland, since 1546, there is a statue known as the "Child Eater." The figure is as puzzling as it is creepy, and no one really knows why it was created. Some think it depicts Kronos, a Greek Titan known for eating his children. Others suggest it's the older brother of Duke Berchtold, the founder of Bern. They say his jealousy drove him crazy, leading him to gobble up the city's children. Whatever its origin, this eerie statue has been giving Swiss children nightmares for almost 500 years!

DEEP WATERS

Champion wakeskater Brian Grubb rode an electric surfboard on a river 100 feet (30.5 m) below the ground!

It was the first time anyone had ever ridden an eFoil underground. An eFoil is a board with an electric propeller that lifts the board and rider above the water for a smooth ride. But even with his high-tech board, Brian's ride through Indiana's Bluespring Caverns was not easy. The passage was narrow, dark, and curvy. The water was almost too shallow in some places. But Brian was up for the challenge! He sped across 2 miles (3.2 km) of the underground river and hit speeds of up to 20 mph (32 kmph)!

CAVE ESCAPE

After robbing a gas station in Hubei Province, China, of $23 in 2009, Liu Moufu spent the next 14 years hiding from police in a remote mountain cave. In 2023, tired of living as a hermit, he turned himself in to the authorities.

ECO HEARSE

Undertaker Isabelle Plumereau rides a bicycle hearse around Paris, France, to promote green funerals. She offers a service where the coffin is transported on a specially designed cargo bicycle instead of in a motor vehicle.

HAIRY SPONGE

Hairdressers and barbers in Belgium collect cut hair from their customers to help protect the environment. The hair is recycled into square mats, which are then placed in drains to soak up any pollution before it reaches a river. A mat using 2.2 pounds (1 kg) of hair can absorb 2 gallons (8 liters) of oil and hydrocarbons.

GREEN GLARE

A storm that hit Darwin, Australia, in October 2022 produced visible green lightning instead of blue. Flashes of green lightning are rarely seen because they usually occur inside clouds. They may be caused either by the colors of a sunset or by oxygen in the atmosphere being activated by the electric charge along the lightning bolt.

THANKFUL VILLAGE

Despite its violent-sounding name, Upper Slaughter in England is one of only 14 English and Welsh villages where no residents were killed in either of the world wars. Upper Slaughter sent 25 people in World War I and 36 in World War II, and they all returned home.

MARBLE MUSEUM

Lee's Legendary Marbles and Collectibles museum in York, Nebraska, displays part of owner Lee Batterton's collection of over one million marbles, some dating back to the early nineteenth century. He started collecting marbles as a boy in the 1930s.

FISH SHOWER

It has rained fish on the remote desert town of Lajamanu in Australia's Northern Territory four times in the last 50 years. In February 2023, live fish fell from the sky during a storm even though the nearest body of water is many miles away.

MANE ATTRACTION

Towering over a canal in Falkirk, Scotland, are two giant glowing horse heads! Called *The Kelpies*, they are named after horse-like mythical creatures from Irish and Scottish legends. The steel sculpture is the work of Scottish artist Andy Scott. He made it in honor of the horses that played a large role in the area's history. Each head weighs around 330 tons and stands nearly 100 feet (30.5 m) tall—as high as a 10-story building!

Fierce & FURRY

In Bulgaria, furry (and often horned) Kukeri dance through town to ward off evil spirits!

Kukeri are part of ancient rituals with origins that are too far back to pinpoint. The tradition sees men and women dress up in costumes of furs, animal skins, and masks. Around their waists they wear big bells, some of which weigh up to 220 pounds (100 kg)! The costumes and bells are often passed down through families for generations. In the past, the Kukeri would go to people's houses. Now, they mostly perform at festivals and events to welcome the changing seasons.

THAT'S A HEAVY LOAD!

SCARY FUN!

UNIQUE BEAK

This bird's beak isn't broken! Crossbills are a type of finch that look like they have an overbite and an underbite at the same time. But this bizarre beak is really an amazing tool. It is perfect for picking seeds out of tree cones, even ones that are still tightly closed! This special ability means crossbills are able to feed themselves and their chicks even in the dead of winter. And that's nothing to be cross about!

SELF LOVE

An endangered bush stone-curlew flew hundreds of miles across Australia in search of a mate—but instead ended up staring at its own reflection in the window of a hardware store in Evans Head, New South Wales.

RADIATION GUARD

Green tree frogs living in Ukraine near the Chernobyl nuclear power plant, which exploded in 1986, have turned black to help combat the effects of radiation. Dark coloration is known to offer greater protection against radiation.

BLOOD BROTHERS

Vampire bats will share a meal of blood with other bats in the same family or ones with which they have developed a close bond. Since the bats need to drink blood every 48 hours to survive, they will regurgitate their blood meal so that it can be divided among family and close friends.

BLUE FLESH

The lingcod, a fish native to the west coast of North America, usually has white-hued flesh but, for reasons unknown, up to one in four specimens has bright blue flesh.

BULLET PROOF

An armadillo's shell is so hard it can deflect a bullet. A man in Texas discovered this when he tried to shoot an armadillo, only for the bullet to bounce off the shell and hit the man in the face. Although he was wounded and airlifted to the hospital, he survived.

HOUSE IN THE CLOUDS

Appearing to float above the trees, the House in the Clouds in Thorpeness, England, used to be a water tower. Some thought it was ugly, so builders turned the tower into a home! At 70 feet (21 m) high, visitors get amazing views. Inside are five bedrooms, three bathrooms, a drawing room, and a special room that belonged to a water tank. The House in the Clouds was built in 1923 and is a protected building for its history of providing water to the local area.

A HOUSE WITH A VIEW!

Block's
BALLOONS

Dan Block will *blow* you away with his unique style of creating balloon animals!

The Austin, Texas, performer starts by threading the balloon into his nostril, through his sinus cavity, and out of his mouth. Then, he places an air pump in his nose and inflates the balloon. At this point, Dan knots and twists the elastic tube into that classic balloon-dog shape—with its head coming out of Dan's nose and the body out of his mouth!

DAN CAN MAKE A BALLOON DOG IN UNDER 45 SECONDS!

REACH FOR THE SKY

The Australian peacock spider is crawling with colors! The peacock spider is covered in a fluorescent fuzz that gives off bright hues. The spider is known for its mating dance. Males will raise two legs high into the air as a way to attract the attention of females. This spider is sure to catch the eye—with its vibrant colors and dance moves!

NANO NEST

The nest of the vervain hummingbird, which lives in Hispaniola and Jamaica, measures only 0.75 inches (1.8 cm) wide and 1.2 inches (3 cm) deep—about half the size of a walnut shell. The bird typically lays two eggs, each around 0.39 inches (1 cm) long.

GENEROUS GIFT

Rhesus macaque monkeys own 32 acres (13 hectares) of land in the village of Upla in India's Maharashtra state. The villagers admire the local population of around 100 monkeys so much that they registered the farmland in the animals' name.

SPIDER BOOM

Around 50,000 species of spider have already been discovered—and experts believe that in less than 100 years another 50,000 spider species will be identified.

TRANSMITTER TREAT

Scientists in Florida got a surprise when a tracking device from a Burmese python turned up inside another snake. By using X-ray, they discovered that a venomous cottonmouth snake had eaten the Burmese python and its transmitter.

TOP DOG

The African painted dog can run at speeds as high as 37 mph (60 kmph) for up to 3 miles (4.8 km). It catches prey in over 70 percent of its hunts, compared to a lion's average of about 30 percent, making it the world's most successful land hunter.

THE PUMPKIN KING

At Sunnyfields Farm in Southampton, England, over 10,000 pumpkins and squash made a giant Jack Skellington! *The Nightmare Before Christmas* mosaic took 10 farm workers five hours to create. It was about the size of a tennis court! In 2022, the farm crafted a pumpkin Paddington Bear. What'll be next?

FLOATING BRIDGE

RIDING ON THE WAVES!

Winding along a river in China's Hubei province is a floating bridge that you can walk or drive on!

Sometimes called the "Bridge of Dreams," the Shiziguan water highway is about 1,640 feet (500 m) long. It's made of wooden planks, is surrounded by lush forests, and sits at water level. It was built in hopes of giving visitors an up-close view of the area's natural beauty with minimal damage to the environment. Those on foot say that it is like walking on water, while drivers have compared it to surfing!

A speed limit is in place to prevent a wake on the water!

BIG TOP TECH

Established in 1976, Germany's Circus Roncalli has continued to evolve and amaze! With animal welfare in mind, they became the first circus in the world to use holographic creatures in their acts. Multiple projectors bring animals to life alongside Circus Roncalli's marvelous performers!

LOOKS SO REAL!

STRAW & AWE

Whittlesea, England, celebrates the harvest in a bear-y unique way. Meet the Straw Bear! Dressed from head to toe in 70 pounds (31.8 kg) of straw, the Straw Bear leads a parade in the streets the Saturday after Plough Monday—the start of England's farming season. Onlookers dance and march with the Straw Bear, giving him gifts of money and food to ensure a hearty harvest!

Catalog No. 21467

Fingernail Dagger

Fingernail daggers, also called "Garuda's Talons," were rumored to have been worn by members of an organized crime group in India during the fourteenth to nineteenth centuries. The wearer could rip the throats of their victims from behind with one slash of these deadly talons!

GARUDA'S TALONS!

Catalog No. 8247

Prison Money

During World War I and II, both Russian and German prisoner of war camps paid prisoners with currency they created! This currency, which was legal only in their camps, was used mostly to purchase goods in the on-site stores.

Catalog No. 10085

Sawfish Club

Sawfish use their tooth-lined rostrums, or snouts, to locate and dismember their prey. Rostrums are revered throughout the world as a tool for shamans to ward off evil spirits. Tribes in the Philippines, New Guinea, and New Zealand were once known for carrying the spiked clubs into battle as powerful weapons!

Catalog No. 21853

Thumb Crusher

Thumb traps—devices that were used to break someone's fingers—were first used by torturers in medieval Europe to force confessions. This dragon-shaped crusher has three holes—enough to crush most of someone's hand!

THAT'S GOING TO LEAVE A MARK!

TORTURE DEVICE!

Go With the Flow!

WATERFALL OR NOT?

Near the island of Mauritius in the Indian Ocean, there is a giant underwater waterfall! Or so it would seem.

The strange view can only be seen from high in the sky. But there isn't really an underwater river flowing over a cliff on the ocean floor. From the island's shore, there is a steady slope leading out to a sudden, 2.5-mile (4-km) drop. What looks like water going over its edge is actually white sand falling into the abyss. This creates the illusion of an underwater waterfall!

ROOFTOP SUBURB

With a shortage of land to build on, Cosmo Park, a suburb of Jakarta, Indonesia, is located atop a 10-story shopping mall. Cosmo Park has 78 two-story houses, swimming pools, green spaces, a tennis court, and even a network of roads. Residents can drive up via a special ramp. The entire roof is surrounded by a metal fence to stop anyone from accidentally plunging over the sides.

FAKE FUNERAL

A 60-year-old Brazilian man, Baltazar Lemos, faked his own death to see how many people would attend his funeral. He posted a message on social media informing people that he had died, and on January 18, 2023, friends and family gathered in a chapel in his home city of Curitiba to pay their last respects... at which point he stepped out from behind the altar doors, very much alive. The mourners were said to be confused and angry.

LEAP YEAR

As midnight approaches on New Year's Eve in Denmark, people traditionally stand on a chair and leap down to the floor. Danes believe that by spending the last moments of the old year with their feet off the ground, they can jump into the New Year with fresh enthusiasm, leaving any negativity behind.

SPLIT STYLE

Built in the eighteenth century, Castle Ward in County Down, Northern Ireland, is a stately mansion of two halves. The owners, Lord and Lady Bangor, could not agree about style, so they split the house down the middle, internally and externally, to accommodate both their tastes. One half is built in his preferred classic Palladian style, the other in her choice of the more elaborate Gothic style. Shortly after the house was finished, the couple separated.

WEDDING SHOWER

Residents of Gorakhpur, India, tried to solve the drought in the summer of 2022 by "marrying" two frogs—a tradition that is supposed to bring rain. Hundreds of people attended the ceremony, and the following day heavy rain fell in the region for the first time in weeks. In 2019, it rained so much after a similar frog wedding in Bhopal, India, that two months later the frogs were divorced so that the rain would stop.

Model
MATERIAL

Rescue dogs Sookie and Ivy are internet famous for wearing adorable crochet hats!

All of the hats are crocheted by their owner, Jani. Sookie and Ivy first went viral after Jani shared a photo of them wearing broccoli hats. The adorable duo quickly gained an online following and were soon wearing all sorts of handmade headgear! They are most often seen wearing hats shaped like dog-friendly foods. Jani hopes the cute photos teach people not to judge dogs like Sookie and Ivy by their appearance.

SAY "WOOF!"

CHOCOLATE FROG

Deep in the Peruvian Amazon, a frog that looks a lot like a yummy chocolate treat has been found! Nicknamed the tapir frog because of its snout, this burrowing frog has been hiding for ages. While known by locals, it wasn't discovered by scientists until 2022!

SWEET!

TINY SPIDER

The Colombian spider *Patu digua* measures only 0.015 inches (0.37 mm) long, making it about one-fifth the size of a pinhead.

GOLF HAZARD

A western diamondback rattlesnake was discovered in a ball dispenser at a golf driving range in Scottsdale, Arizona.

DARING STUNT

When actor Harold Lloyd hung from the hands of a large clock on the side of an office building high above a busy street in the 1923 silent movie *Safety Last!*, he did so with only eight fingers. He had lost part of his right index finger, his entire right thumb, and part of his palm four years earlier in a stunt that went wrong.

WILLY WONKA

Nick Franklin, from Manchester, England, has collected more than 2,000 items of Willy Wonka memorabilia, including a life-size cutout of actor Gene Wilder—who played Willy Wonka in the 1971 movie—a 10-foot-long (3-m) candy cane from the 2005 film, and 100 different versions of Roald Dahl's *Charlie and the Chocolate Factory* novel.

PAW PATROL

Conan the cat was a stray before he became a security guard! He was adopted by the security team at an office building in Manila, Philippines. Conan wears a security vest during his shifts with the guards, however his work ethic isn't up to snuff. While he dresses for the job, he prefers to take naps or hang out at Starbucks and play with his toys.

CAT BURGLARS BEWARE!

MONSTER TRUCK

FOR REALLY BIG DUMPS!

The BelAZ-75710 is the biggest dump truck in the world!

The huge vehicle is 66 feet (20 m) long, 32 feet (9.8 m) wide, and 27 feet (8.2 m) high. That's as big as two buses placed end to end! Each of its giant tires weighs as much as 5.5 tons. Even when it's empty, the truck weighs 360 tons. The truck isn't just big—it's powerful. It can carry more than 500 tons, which is like lifting 75 elephants at once!

BUBBLY ABODE

The Bubble Palace near Cannes, France, has so many domes that it looks like a bubble bath! Construction of the house, developed by Hungarian architect Antti Lovag, started in 1975. Ancient cave dwellings inspired the building's design, but it is far from primitive. The Bubble Palace has 29 rooms, multiple pools, and its own outdoor auditorium that can seat 500 people!

BURGLAR BLUNDER

A serial burglar in Tulsa, Oklahoma, was identified partly by the distinctive SpongeBob SquarePants shorts and socks that he wore during many of his robberies.

KEY WORD

Rather than asking them to say "cheese," nineteenth-century photographers in the UK encouraged women to say the word "prunes" so that their mouths would look small and refined.

KETCHUP ELVIS

After dunking her last chicken nugget, Lisa Ringsell from Dundee, Scotland, discovered that the leftover tomato ketchup in the pot had formed a shape resembling the face of Elvis Presley.

EXAM ETCHER

A Spanish law student tried to cheat on an exam by painstakingly etching hundreds of essential words into the plastic of 11 pens.

FINGERLESS FOE

Police officers investigating an attempted home invasion in Burlington, North Carolina, found an incriminating piece of evidence at the scene—the suspect's severed finger. The digit was discovered inside a glove, which fell off during a struggle when the homeowner slammed the door shut on the suspect's hand.

POINTY PAIN

After she lived in pain for 11 years, an MRI finally revealed the source. Maria Aderlinda Forero, from Colombia, had a surgical needle and thread inside her body from an operation she had after giving birth to her fourth child.

WEB COUNT

In 2022, there were 1.98 billion websites on the internet—around one website for every four people in the world.

MIRACLE MAN

Australian fitness instructor Phill Zdybel suffered a heart attack while playing basketball and miraculously survived despite dying for 28 minutes.

DEAR DENTURES

A set of false teeth worn by the late Detroit Tigers baseball legend Ty Cobb sold at auction in 2022 for $18,840. Cobb died in 1961.

Cursed Curiosities

There are many items in this world believed to bring bad luck or have magic abilities. Such claims are nearly impossible to confirm, but the stories continue to captivate people to this day. Here are just a few mysterious objects with tales that have taken on a life of their own.

CHILD'S PLAY

In the early 1900s, Robert the Doll was gifted to a boy named Robert "Gene" Otto. Some believe the 3-foot-tall (0.9-m) wooden sailor with black, round eyes and a scarred face is haunted! Gene would have full conversations with the doll, talking for Robert in a distinctly different voice. Gene also claimed the doll was to blame for upturned furniture and broken toys. Today, Robert is on display at the Fort East Martello Museum in Key West, Florida. People claim to have seen the doll move or change facial expressions! Some even send Robert apology letters believing he put a hex on them!

DARE TO STARE!

DEADLY DOLL

According to legend, Haitian President François Duvalier, a.k.a. Papa Doc, once used a voodoo doll against U.S. President John F. Kennedy! Some say Papa Doc stabbed the doll 2,222 times on November 22, 1963—the same day Kennedy died. Today, the doll is on display at Ripley's Believe It or Not! in St. Augustine, Florida. Strange events have been reported there, such as the doll's glass case fogging up as if the doll was breathing! Superstition says not to stare into its eyes or it might haunt you!

HAUNTED HOPE?

HOPELESS DIAMOND

The Hope Diamond was the inspiration behind the Heart of the Ocean—the big, blue jewel in the *Titanic* movie. But instead of love, the Hope Diamond is said to bear a curse that has lasted for generations! The story goes that a French merchant stole the jewel from a Hindu statue in India before selling it to King Louis XIV of France. From there, it's said that many who wore the stone ended up suffering gruesome fates—such as the beheadings of Louis XVI and Marie Antoinette. Today, the Hope Diamond resides at the Smithsonian National Museum of Natural History, where it hopefully won't cost anyone their life.

CURSED RING

Things went downhill for famous 1920s silent film star Rudolph Valentino after he bought the Destiny Ring. The shopkeeper warned him it was cursed, but Rudolph wore the ring anyway in his movies. Not long after, he fell ill and died young— allegedly while wearing the ring. His love, actress Pola Negri, wore the ring next and also became very sick. She gave the jewelry to her friend, singer Russ Colombo, who died soon after! Today, the Destiny Ring is rumored to either be locked away in a Los Angeles bank or stolen.

CURSE OR COINCIDENCE?

" My biggest accomplishment is that I seem to inspire other people.

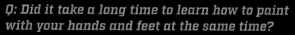

RIPLEY'S EXCLUSIVE

Sketch FLEX

Rajacenna van Dam, from the Netherlands, can use both hands and feet to create eight detailed drawings—at the same time!

Rajacenna started making realistic art when she was 16 years old. Since then, her work has been seen all around the world. In 2019, she challenged herself to draw with both hands. A few years later, she added both feet into the mix! To understand how she can do so many things at once, Rajacenna had a brain scan called an electroencephalogram (EEG). It showed that the right and left sides of her brain are three times more connected than average! Ripley's spoke with Rajacenna to ask her about her rare talent. Check out what she had to say!

Q: Did it take a long time to learn how to paint with your hands and feet at the same time?

A: Not really, because I just tried it right away. I started painting an eye and when I found out I could do that, I tried six portraits. In the beginning it felt a bit weird and I had to get used to it. But the more I did it, the more comfortable it was to hold the brush between my toes. It was interesting to watch myself slowly make progress with my feet and to learn something entirely new. I don't really think about it. I just sit to draw and paint.

Q: What techniques do you use when painting multiple pieces at once?

A: A lot of time and patience goes into the process of working on the paintings. When I work on eight artworks simultaneously, I have to divide my focus and constantly switch my focus back and forth. And try to not think too much about it. Before I start such projects, I make sure to quiet my mind and that helps a lot.

Q: What do you consider your biggest accomplishment?

A: For me, the process of making artwork is the most important thing, and my biggest accomplishment is that I seem to inspire other people.

Q: Who or what inspires you?

A: The people I choose to paint are all interesting and creative icons. They inspire me all in a different way and also because they are different in their looks, it is more of a challenge to me.

Q: Is there anything you would like to let our audience know?

A: In general, I hope to inspire people to be creative in any area. And to show that if you are patient, make the effort to learn or do something, and make it more and more difficult for yourself, that you can sometimes do more than you think.

AMAZING TALENT!

MULTITASKING QUEEN!

Catalog No. 175661

Strawberry Field Brick

Strawberry Field was originally an opulent mansion built in 1870 for a wealthy shipping mogul! It was sold to the Salvation Army around 1936 and converted into an orphanage for girls. As a child, John Lennon would often sneak into their garden to escape his tumultuous home situation. This brick is from the Strawberry Field house, which eventually inspired Lennon's song, "Strawberry Fields Forever."

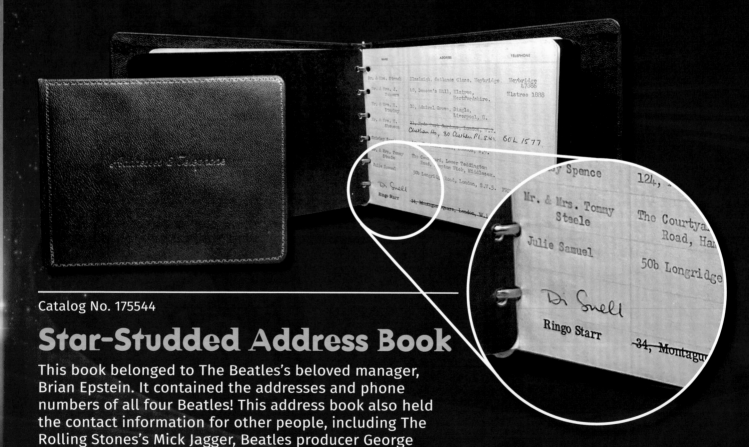

Catalog No. 175544

Star-Studded Address Book

This book belonged to The Beatles's beloved manager, Brian Epstein. It contained the addresses and phone numbers of all four Beatles! This address book also held the contact information for other people, including The Rolling Stones's Mick Jagger, Beatles producer George Martin, and more.

AN EARLY
APPLE
WATCH?

Catalog No. 175659

Beatles Apple Watch

This extremely rare watch was sold at The Beatles's Apple Boutique in London, England, in 1967. The boutique was only open for eight months before closing because it wasn't profitable. They did make some products before they closed for good, including this suede-banded watch printed with The Beatles's iconic green Apple Corps logo on the face.

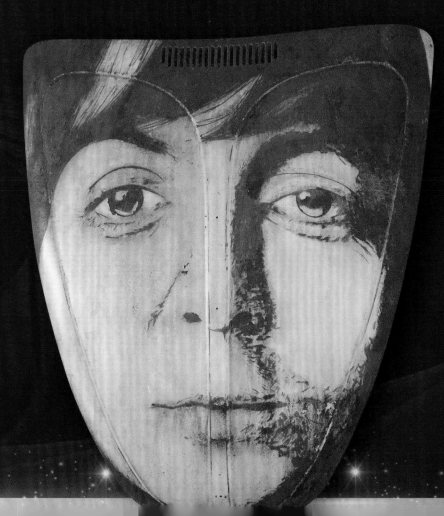

Catalog No. 170641

Beatle Beetle

Michael Stodola uses rust to create his works of art! He uses a mix of chemicals that rust fresh metal quickly and a head-on picture of his subject for reference. Believe it or not, the first car portrait he did was of Abraham Lincoln on a 1975 Lincoln!

MIGHTY MARBLE

Weighing an incredible 12,500 pounds (5,670 kg) and towering 17 feet (5 m) tall, Michelangelo's *David* is a true giant in the world of art!

How do you clean something as tall as an adult giraffe? Ask Eleonora Pucci, a restorer who has the high-pressure job of cleaning this 500-plus-year-old masterpiece. To keep *David* looking his best, she uses fine brushes, a vacuum, and soft fabrics to gently remove dust and dirt. She also carefully climbs two-story-high scaffolding to reach *David*'s famous face! Any small mistake could damage one of the world's greatest sculptures, so her job takes a lot of skill!

DAVID'S TWIN IN FLORIDA

Ripley's Believe It or Not! in St. Augustine, Florida, is home to one of only two exact replicas of *David*! Modestly hidden behind hedges, this twin is made of pure Carrara marble from Tuscany, Italy—the same quarry where Michelangelo acquired the marble for his masterpiece!

FAITHFUL FRIEND

When 84-year-old Gregorio Romero got lost in the desert, his pet dog tracked him for nearly 2 miles (3.2 km) through ravines and hills. Gregorio had been missing for a week when El Palomo led the rescue party to the exact spot where Gregorio had become stranded, near his home in Moctezuma, Mexico. The brown dog then waited outside his owner's hospital room for two days while he was being treated.

HIPPO HORROR

Two-year-old Iga Paul survived being half-swallowed by a hippo. The boy was playing near his home in Kasese, Uganda, when he was snatched head-first by the hippo. It then tried to swallow him, but the hippo was forced to regurgitate the child unharmed after stones were thrown at it.

MEGA QUAKE

The 1755 Great Lisbon earthquake destroyed 85 percent of the Portuguese city's buildings and caused a tsunami so powerful that its large waves hit the coast of Brazil more than 4,300 miles (7,000 km) away on the other side of the Atlantic Ocean.

NEVER-ENDING NAILS

Diana Armstrong has fingernails with a combined length of just over 42 feet 10 inches (13 m)—longer than a bus. Her longest nail is her right thumbnail at just over 4.67 feet (1.4 m). She hasn't cut her fingernails for over 25 years, and their extreme length means she no longer drives or wears clothes with zippers. It takes her five hours to file and polish her nails, using up to 20 bottles of nail polish at a time.

EAR-MAZING

Africa's bat-eared fox loves to eat dung beetles, and its very large ears give it such good hearing that it can actually hear the beetle eggs hatching inside balls of dung.

PUPPY POWER

A bulldog puppy named Harley nearly chewed off his sleeping owner's big toe—without him feeling a thing. Woken by his screaming wife, David Lindsay discovered his toe covered in blood and his foot was completely numb. Scans showed that he had two blocked arteries, and the lack of blood flow to his foot could have led to the removal of his entire leg if it hadn't been discovered so early.

BUSY BEE

A queen bee can lay up to 2,500 eggs in a single day—twice her body weight.

BARK RANGER

Gracie the border collie is employed by Montana's Glacier National Park as a "bark ranger"—a dog that helps to herd goats, deer, sheep, and other wildlife away from areas where there are a lot of visitors.

FURRY NIGHT

Meet Van Gogh, the one-eared pup that paints with his tongue! Named after nineteenth-century artist Vincent van Gogh, who also had just one ear, the boxer–pit bull mix has made more than 150 paintings! He did it with the help of Jaclyn Gartner, founder of Happily Furever After Rescue in Connecticut. First, a canvas is covered with blobs of paint and placed inside a plastic bag. The outside of the bag is then covered with peanut butter. Finally, Van Gogh licks the tasty treat off of the bag, smearing the paint. Et voilà—art is born! In 2023, his version of *The Starry Night* by the real Vincent van Gogh sold at auction for $10,000!

Winged WARRIORS

Climbing teacher Joos Habraken of Ghent, Belgium, turns body parts from dead insects into fierce, mythical warriors!

Each creation uses dozens of pieces and can take Joos, a former taxidermist, up to 40 hours to make. He gives them all their own name and special backstory. Among his favorites is Ruja the fungus farmer. Her grasshopper head is covered in hair made of bug legs! She wears a shiny green dress of dragonfly and beetle wings. And she holds a staff made from a stick insect and a beetle's thorax. Joos hopes his art shows people how beautiful nature can be.

DRAGONFLY WING SWORD!

Hanzō the swordsman.

Brokkr the goldsmith.

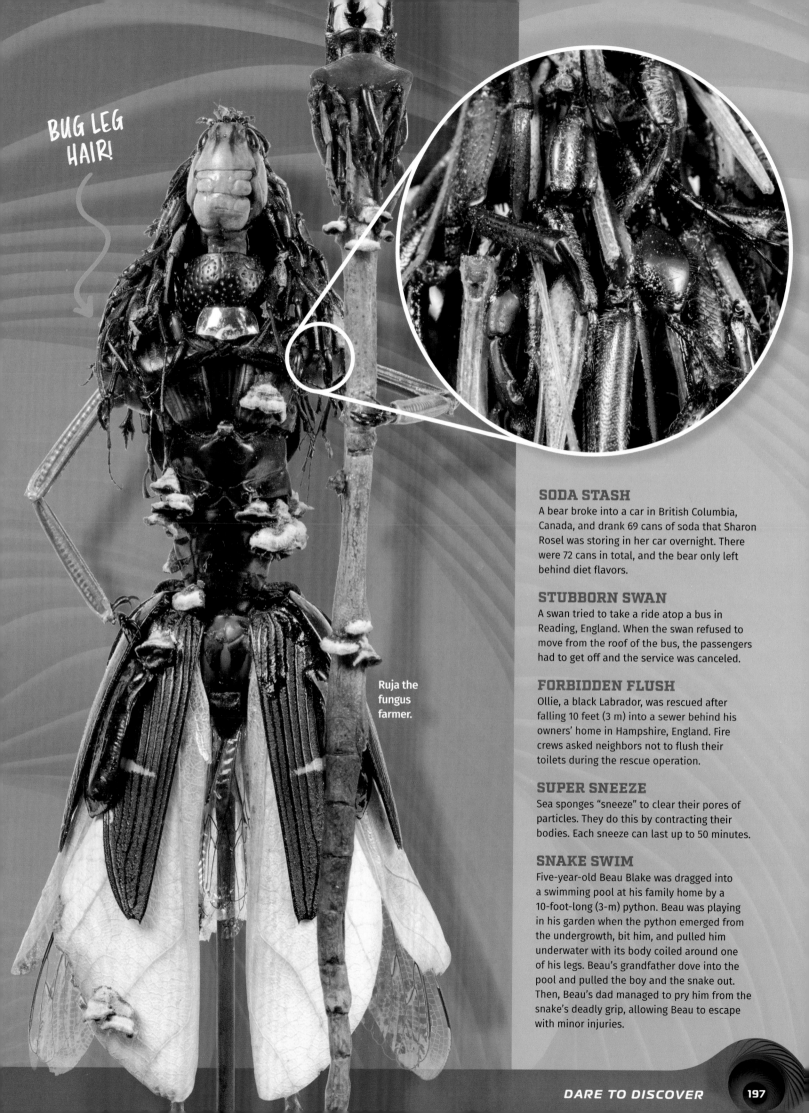

BUG LEG HAIR!

Ruja the fungus farmer.

SODA STASH

A bear broke into a car in British Columbia, Canada, and drank 69 cans of soda that Sharon Rosel was storing in her car overnight. There were 72 cans in total, and the bear only left behind diet flavors.

STUBBORN SWAN

A swan tried to take a ride atop a bus in Reading, England. When the swan refused to move from the roof of the bus, the passengers had to get off and the service was canceled.

FORBIDDEN FLUSH

Ollie, a black Labrador, was rescued after falling 10 feet (3 m) into a sewer behind his owners' home in Hampshire, England. Fire crews asked neighbors not to flush their toilets during the rescue operation.

SUPER SNEEZE

Sea sponges "sneeze" to clear their pores of particles. They do this by contracting their bodies. Each sneeze can last up to 50 minutes.

SNAKE SWIM

Five-year-old Beau Blake was dragged into a swimming pool at his family home by a 10-foot-long (3-m) python. Beau was playing in his garden when the python emerged from the undergrowth, bit him, and pulled him underwater with its body coiled around one of his legs. Beau's grandfather dove into the pool and pulled the boy and the snake out. Then, Beau's dad managed to pry him from the snake's deadly grip, allowing Beau to escape with minor injuries.

Kriss Kyle took BMX to new heights by riding his bike in a skate park soaring 2,000 feet (609 m) above the ground!

For a stunt Kyle called "Don't Look Down," he did bike tricks in a skate park bowl hanging from a hot-air balloon. The unprecedented feat took place over Cotswolds in Wiltshire, England. Don't worry—Kyle wore a parachute to be safe. Other considerations had to be made, as well. The skate park was made of carbon fiber in order to be light enough to be carried by the balloon. The weather also had to be perfect, forcing Kyle to wait an entire year to ride!

RAD RIDE

SKATE PARK IN THE SKY!

SWIFT SKIP
Gbenga Ezekiel, a 16-year-old student at Ijapo High School in Nigeria, skipped rope 265 times on one leg in just a minute.

PERFECT PANTS
American sailor Larry Savadkin survived the sinking of the USS *Tang* off Taiwan during World War II by inflating his pants and using them as a life jacket. After reaching the ocean surface, he took off his pants and tied the legs and waist to fashion an impromptu life vest.

CROCHET-MAS TREE
A group of 70 women in Lisbon, Portugal, with ages ranging from 11 to 88, crocheted a 55.7-foot-tall (17-m) Christmas tree. The tree, which was the height of a five-story apartment block, consisted of 7,200 squares of crochet.

BLINDFOLD BALL
Nine-year-old Henry Speedwell, a student at Mount Greenwood Elementary School in Chicago, dribbled a basketball for 1 hour 20 minutes 1 second while wearing a blindfold.

CANYON CROSSING
Ninety-one-year-old John Jepkema crossed the Grand Canyon rim-to-rim on foot, completing the 24-mile (38-km) trek in five days. He started on the North Rim and descended 6,000 feet (1,829 m) to the bottom of the canyon before climbing 4,500 feet (1,372 m) to the South Rim.

LUCKY LEAVES
Gabriella Gerhardt from Wisconsin has a collection of nearly 119,000 four-leaf clovers, which she has been seeking out since 2010. Gabriella also has more than 1,400 six-leaf clovers and 200 seven-leaf clovers.

STICKY SKIN
Jamie Keeton, of Kenosha, Wisconsin, is able to stick 10 cans to his head simultaneously using only air suction! Objects such as water bottles, pencils, and cell phones stick to his skin because his skin absorbs more oxygen than most people's. In fact, his oxygen levels are 23 percent higher than average.

Touching TECH

Fabric, air, and computers have been combined to create huge, huggable robots!

The soft robots are interactive and can show different moods. Some are as tall as a two-story building! They were made by Air Giants and the Bristol Interaction Group. The robots' movements are made by changing the amount of air in their bodies. Since they don't have any hard or dangerous parts, the lifelike creatures are safe for people of all ages and abilities to touch and play with!

CUTE AND CUDDLY ROBOTS!

SEASIDE SKELETON

There is a 426.5-foot-long (130-m) metal snake skeleton on a beach in France! Titled *Serpent D'Océan*, the slithering sculpture was created by Chinese artist Huang Yong Ping. It looks as if it's rising and sinking with the ocean's waves—like a real sea creature! The giant piece of art isn't just for looks, though. The *Serpent D'Océan* was also made as a reminder to take care of our oceans and the animals living in them.

WASHED-UP SEA MONSTER?

LOST RING

In 2017, Joey Lykins lost his nose piercing, only to find it five years later lodged in his left lung. He went to the hospital with a bad cough and an X-ray showed the cause—his missing septum ring was stuck in his lung. It had probably fallen off while he was asleep and he unknowingly inhaled it.

BABY MIX-UP

Jim Mitchell and Margaret Rafferty were briefly mixed up as babies at a hospital in Lennoxtown, Scotland, in 1952. Nurses handed them to the wrong mothers, both of whom were called Margaret. They went on to lead separate lives for 18 years until they met again when two of their friends married each other. Jim asked Margaret out at the wedding reception, and two years later, in 1972, they got married. In 2022, they celebrated their golden wedding anniversary.

SUPERSTITIOUS SERENA

U.S. tennis star Serena Williams always bounces the ball five times before a first serve and twice before a second serve.

RESTAURANT RUSH

On October 26, 2022, food enthusiast Eric Finkelstein dined at 18 of New York City's Michelin-starred restaurants in only 11 hours. He ate one dish in each, sometimes finishing in less than two minutes, and spent a total of $494 (not including tips). He consumed an estimated 5,000 calories—double the recommended daily intake for an adult male.

CRIMINAL COPS

A gang in Banka, India, ran a fake police station out of a hotel for eight months. Wearing realistic uniforms, they set up the fake station 1,600 feet (500 m) from the real one and scammed hundreds of people.

ENORMOUS ERASER

Japanese company Seed launched the Radar S-10000—a $100 eraser that measures 11 × 4.3 inches (27.6 × 14 cm) and weighs over 5 pounds (2.2 kg), making it 200 times heavier than a standard eraser.

TRIPLE BIRTHDAY

Married couple Cassidy and Dylan Scott were both born on December 18—a date they now share with their daughter, born in 2022, beating odds of 133,000 to one.

FROGGY FRIEND

Nineteenth-century Norwegian composer and pianist Edvard Grieg always kept a small, rubber frog in his pocket. Before each performance he would pat the frog on the head for good luck and inspiration.

House of Cards

There are monsters in the hills of Tuscany. Some are painted in pinks, oranges, and blues. Others are decked out like disco balls!

French artist Niki de Saint Phalle spent over 20 years of her life on the Tarot Garden. Inspired by tarot cards illustrated for insight and wisdom, her whimsical creations are larger than life. They are so big that Niki lived inside one during construction! Step inside and you'll be in awe of this completely mirrored space. Bold and covered in colorful mosaics, her art continues to inspire and amaze!

INSPIRED BY TAROT CARDS!

ROOMS COVERED IN MIRRORS!

CREATIVE, WHIMSICAL ART!

Catalog No. 14624

Monkey Skull Bowl

This bowl is made from a real monkey skull! Skull bowls, called kapalas, were sometimes used in Tibetan monasteries. They were filled with dough cakes or wine to symbolize flesh or blood and offered to the gods.

Catalog No. 166822

Oracle's Crown

This shaman's crown from the early twentieth century is made from pure silver! The five points on this crown may represent the five poisons, or kleshas: anger, ignorance, pride, desire, and jealousy. Tibetan oracles and shamans often wore ornate headdresses during rituals and ceremonies.

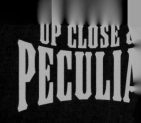

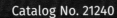

Catalog No. 21240

Human Skull Coffee Pot

In Tibet, skulls were often used to create objects and celebrate the life of a deceased loved one. This coffee urn is made from a genuine human skull and is carved with images of gods and demons.

Catalog No. 173797

Sacred Turtle Shell

Traditionally, skull bowls were used to make offerings to the deities of Hindu India and Buddhist Tibet. In more recent years, this ritual of tantra-practicing monks has been performed using bowls made from other sources such as animal skulls or, in this case, a turtle's shell.

World THOR

Thor Pedersen traveled to every country in the world—without flying in an airplane!

The Danish explorer began his journey in 2013 and traveled an amazing 223,072 miles (359,000 km) in total. He used donations to pay for his trip on boats, buses, and trains for over 10 years. Thor rode 351 buses and 158 trains; he spent 54 hours on a bus in Brazil and five days on a train in Russia! On May 23, 2023, Thor reached the last country on his list: the Maldives. To complete his adventure, Thor returned to Denmark on July 26, 2023, where his journey began.

Thor in Hong Kong in 2020.

Thor in Mongolia in 2018.

Thor with camels in Ethiopia in 2017.

ON A CARGO SHIP IN FIJI!

SMALL WORLD

While talking with her writing professor at the University of Rhode Island, Amanda Birch discovered that not only did the professor live in the same Vermont town in which Amanda's mother had grown up, but in the very same house.

SELLING SCAM

When a couple from Ontario returned home after a long business trip, they discovered that their house had been sold and new owners had moved in. A man and a woman had impersonated the homeowners, hired a real estate agent, and listed the property using fake IDs.

SPECIAL SNEAKER

Dutch beer company Heineken teamed up with LA shoe designer Dominic Ciambrone to create a limited edition sneaker with real beer inside the transparent sole and a removable bottle opener built into the shoe's tongue.

SPOON SCARE

UK musician Liam Payne, who was once a member of boy band One Direction, has koutaliaphobia—a fear of spoons.

IMPROMPTU GAME

The winner of stage four of the 2022 Tour of Slovenia bicycle race was decided by a game of rock, paper, scissors. Teammates Tadej Pogačar and Rafal Majka were a long way ahead of the chasing pack, so in the final stretch, they slowed down and took their hands off the handlebars to play a quick game of rock, paper, scissors. Majka's paper trumped Pogačar's rock, so he crossed the finish line first.

GADGET GOODBYE

Lin Xi runs a gadget funeral service in China where people can have their old or broken devices—including cell phones and watches—preserved forever in glass frames as souvenirs.

LEAD CHEAT

Fishermen Jacob Runyan and Chase Cominsky were disqualified from the 2022 Lake Erie Walleye Trail tournament after officials found that lead balls and fillets of other fish had been inserted into the fish they caught. The prize for heaviest fish at the Ohio contest was $28,760.

MONEY MAKER

As a child, Argentine soccer star Diego Maradona lived in poverty, so he earned money by selling the discarded foil from cigarette packets.

FAMILY CONNECTION

During the U.S. Civil War, John Wilkes Booth's elder brother, Edwin, saved Abraham Lincoln's son, Robert, from falling under a train at a station in Jersey City, New Jersey. A few months later on April 14, 1865, John Wilkes Booth assassinated President Abraham Lincoln.

SANTA'S SUMMIT

In Switzerland, artist Gerry Hofstetter projected a huge Santa Claus onto a mountain! The colorful image covered a whopping 301,390 square feet (28,000 sq m) of the Swiss mountain Rochers-de-Naye—that's as big as five soccer fields! Creating the massive Santa wasn't easy. Gerry had to shine the image from almost 1.5 miles (2.4 km) away to make it appear large enough. He also had to deal with clouds and light from the moon. The project was a success in the end, and Gerry brought a festive spirit to the mountain!

Grass BRIDGE

The Q'eswachaka grass bridge has been rebuilt by hand every summer for more than 500 years!

The 91-foot-long (28-m) suspension bridge spans the Apurímac River near Huinchiri, Peru. The Q'eswachaka is one of the last remaining handwoven bridges from the Inka Empire. It is rebuilt every year to keep it safe to cross. Locals use traditional weaving techniques to twist and braid grass into sturdy ropes that replace the old ones. Incredibly, bridge is completely rebuilt in just three days!

BUILT IN THREE DAYS!

THE PERFECT PITCH!

MESSI MEADOW

Crop farmer Maximiliano Spinazze planted his cornfield in Los Condores, Argentina, so that when it grew, it formed a giant, 124-acre (50-hectare) image of the nation's 2022 World Cup hero, soccer star Lionel Messi.

SOUVENIR SPOONS

Cammie Pohl, from Davenport, Iowa, has a collection of more than 12,400 souvenir spoons commemorating famous people, places, and events. Her collection began with a set of 1904 St. Louis World's Fair spoons gifted to her by her great-grandmother.

SUPER STOP

When the driver of his school bus suddenly lost consciousness at the wheel, 13-year-old Dillon Reeves saved his 66 Michigan schoolmates by steering the vehicle to safety. Seeing the driver pass out, Dillon rushed to the front, took control, stopped the bus from veering into traffic, and calmly brought it to a halt.

HIGH CLIFF

The cliff face called Verona Rupes on Miranda, one of Uranus's moons, is 12.5 miles (20 km) high—more than 10 times the depth of the Grand Canyon. Given the low gravity on Miranda, it would take a person 12 minutes to fall from the top of the cliff to the bottom.

TENS OF TOWERS

There are more than 50 replicas of the famous Eiffel Tower of Paris, France, located across the world—among them are towers in Tokyo, Japan; Sydney, Australia; and Gomez Palacio, Mexico. There are at least nine in the U.S. alone, including in Paris, Michigan; Paris, Tennessee; and Paris, Texas.

PRESERVED POMPEII

Covered and preserved by volcanic ash, the city of Pompeii is a unique treasure trove! Amazing finds like these give us a glimpse into daily life in the ancient city.

Guard Dog Sign: Even 2,000 years ago, humans had guard dogs! This tile floor found in Pompeii features a protective pup and text that reads "Cave Canem," meaning "Beware of the dog" in Latin. The dog even has a red leash!

Snack Bars: A thermopolium was a snack bar or fast-food stand located at a busy spot in the city. Some were even covered in pictures of animals thought to be on the menu!

THESE RUINS ROCK!

Helpful Horse: This horse was wearing a saddle and harness, seemingly ready to help people escape, before being buried by ash when Mount Vesuvius erupted in 79 AD.

Bread Loaves: In the city ruins, archaeologists found ovens with bread still inside! The panis quadratus, or sourdough bread, was round with a hole in the middle and cut into eight pieces.

WAR FILMS

Before finding success as an author of children's books, Dr. Seuss wrote propaganda films for the U.S. Army during World War II.

BRIDGE DUETS

Los Angeles musician Nate Mercereau released an album featuring music from San Francisco's Golden Gate Bridge. In high winds, the bridge made a humming sound so loud that it could be heard 3 miles (4.8 km) away.

AMAZON ORDEAL

Jhonattan Acosta from Bolivia survived 31 days lost in the Amazon jungle by drinking rainwater collected in his shoes and by eating worms and insects.

SECRET SNACKS

The deep pockets of Draco Malfoy's robes were sewn shut after filming the third Harry Potter movie because English actor Tom Felton, who played Malfoy, kept sneaking snacks onto the set.

LOTTERY CARDS

James Owen Thomas, from Yorkshire, England, creates colorful artworks out of old lottery scratchcards. He was inspired when he saw a discarded scratchcard floating in a puddle of water and noticed how the sunlight made its colors glisten. His mosaic-style collages depict wildlife and scenes from the English countryside.

SWEET DEAL

In 1984, James Cameron, who was then a little-known Canadian director, sold the rights to his script for the original *Terminator* film to producer Gale Anne Hurd for $1—on the condition that he was to direct it. The movie went on to gross $78.3 million at the box office.

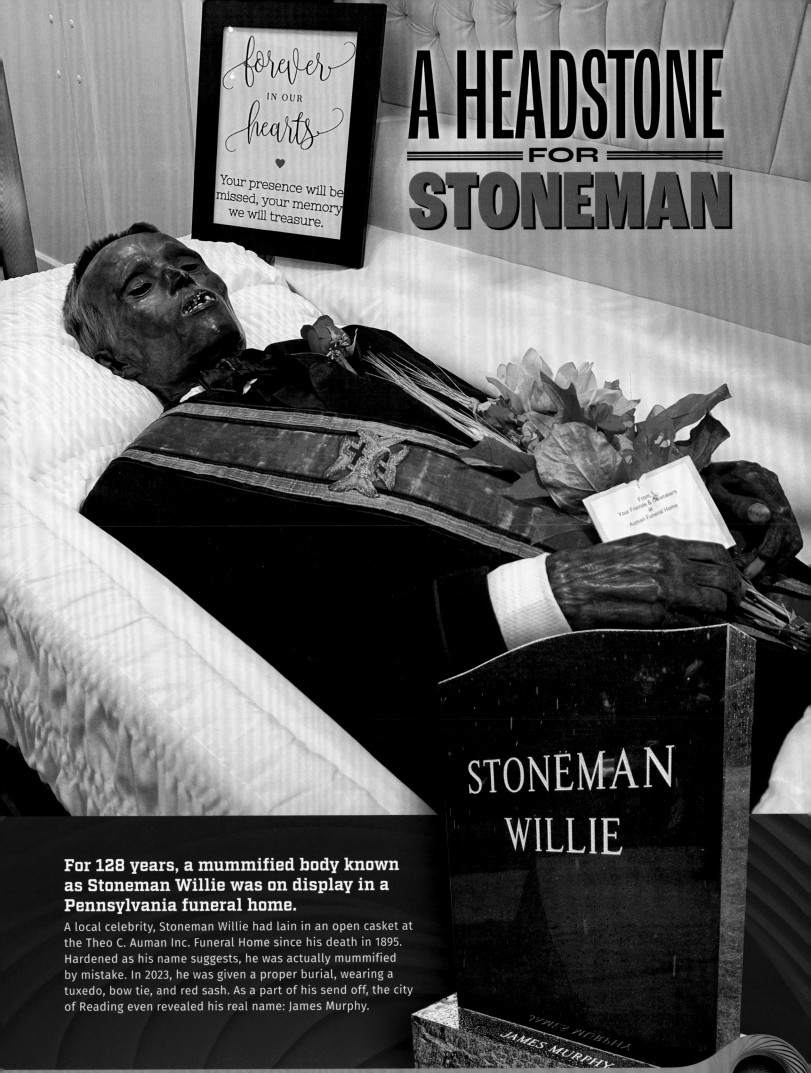

forever
IN OUR
hearts.
❤
Your presence will be missed, your memory we will treasure.

A HEADSTONE
FOR
STONEMAN

From
Your Friends & Caretakers
at
Auman Funeral Home

STONEMAN
WILLIE

For 128 years, a mummified body known as Stoneman Willie was on display in a Pennsylvania funeral home.

A local celebrity, Stoneman Willie had lain in an open casket at the Theo C. Auman Inc. Funeral Home since his death in 1895. Hardened as his name suggests, he was actually mummified by mistake. In 2023, he was given a proper burial, wearing a tuxedo, bow tie, and red sash. As a part of his send off, the city of Reading even revealed his real name: James Murphy.

JAMES MURPHY

Scoot Scoot

Legendary motorcycle racers, brothers Marc and Álex Márquez, took to the streets with a playful nod to scooter culture in Thailand.

Competing in Buriram, Thailand, the two raced on scooters while balancing massive loads. In the first race, they each skillfully balanced 17 bags of Thai silk that weighed over 330 pounds (150 kg) and stretched over 13 feet (4 m) wide! In their second race, they took on more than 200 baskets. Scooters are a common sight in the country, used to transport goods around town—but we're not talking a pizza or two. Scooters can be seen stacked with sacks, brimming with boxes, and piled up with pretty much anything!

NO SEAGULLS ALLOWED!

EAGLE EYE

Corey Grieveson of North Yorkshire, England, has a pretty fly job. He patrols the seaside town of Whitby dressed up as an eagle! He does it to stop seagulls from stealing fish and chips from people. He runs around flapping his wings and squawking at the pesky birds until they fly off. In addition to his hourly wages and tips, Corey's odd job has also earned him some fame. Tourists love him and often ask him for photos. But being a local celebrity means Corey is bound to have some haters—mostly seagulls, who seem to get their revenge by pooping on his car!

HAND IN HALF

Marcelo de Souza Ribeiro, from Brazil, has had surgery to split his left hand between the middle and ring finger in a quest to become alien-like. He has also had the index finger on his right hand chopped off at the knuckle. Marcelo has spent more than $37,000 on body art, including fanged metal teeth, skin implants, a split tongue, and more than 1,500 tattoos inked across 98 percent of his body.

CHIEFS COLLECTIBLES

For 50 years, Curt Herrman has collected more than 1,300 pieces of memorabilia related to the Kansas City Chiefs football team—including cookie jars, doormats, a clock, a bird house, and even a Chiefs trash can.

DANCING FOR DAYS

Friends Claire Harris and Kate Strong line danced around Australia in 2022—traveling 27,961 miles (45,000 km), spending 273 days on the road, and dancing with 2,800 people.

SURF MARATHON

In March 2023, Australian Blake Johnston surfed for 40 hours straight at Cronulla Beach, New South Wales, and rode more than 700 waves.

SEAT FEAT

Jonathan Burns can squeeze his entire body through a toilet seat! It is one of the many stunts he performs as a professional entertainer. Jonathan's career can be traced back to when he started learning magic tricks at 12 years old. But his ability to bend has always been a part of him. Jonathan has a connective tissue disorder that helps him flex his body to the extreme. "Rather than hide it or let that hold me back," he says, "I've used my genetic mutation to entertain people around the world." Today, Jonathan combines comedy, magic, and contortion into one-of-a-kind acts that leave you on the edge of your (hopefully not toilet) seat!

INDIANA BONES

Meet Indiana Bones, a cool furry friend of creative groomer Alicia Mulac!

Alicia created the tribute to movie adventurer Indiana Jones by shaving and coloring a dog's fur to look like items from the films. Using dog-safe dye, she even gave the pup a hat and turned his tail into a whip! Oddly enough, this isn't the only connection Indiana Jones has with dogs. The series's creator, George Lucas, named the character after his pet Alaskan malamute. The third movie, *Indiana Jones and the Last Crusade*, nods to this fact by revealing that Jones's real first name is actually Henry and that Indiana was his dog's name!

THE CANINE CRUSADER!

ROCKY RELICS

The Rock-Hewn Churches of Lalibela, Ethiopia, are carved out of a mountain! The 11 churches were built during the twelfth and thirteenth centuries. They include doors, windows, roofs, and ditches to help keep the area dry. There are also hidden caves and tunnels to connect the churches! Inside each building is a replica of the Ark of the Covenant, plus other religious artifacts, only for priests to see.

CUDDLY CROC

Jonathan Araiza has a pet crocodile, Gamora, who knows how to climb the stairs of his house and even sleeps next to him in bed. Jonathan allows the croc, who acts like a dog and loves to be kissed and cuddled, to roam freely about his house in San Luis Potosi, Mexico.

SUPER SMELL

A male emperor moth can smell a female emperor moth from up to 6.8 miles (11 km) away.

MOVIE MOOSE

A moose wandered into a movie theater in Kenai, Alaska, and started eating popcorn. Before leaving, the animal rooted around the contents of a trash can, including the remains of a McDonald's Happy Meal.

NO-RIFT GIFT

To persuade the female scorpion fly not to kill him during the mating process, the male sometimes presents her with a gift—a dead insect or saliva ball.

PARTIAL TO PEE

Mountain goats in Washington State's Olympic National Park have developed a taste for drinking human urine left behind by hikers.

CROC KING

Doogie Lish Sandtiger from Connecticut has a collection of more than 2,100 pairs of Croc shoes. Known as the "Croc King," he got his first pair of rubber clogs when he was 16 and has been collecting them for over 17 years. He wears several pairs a day but uses the more colorful ones as decor around the house. Among his prized possessions is a pair of fried chicken–scented Crocs.

NOT YOUR TYPICAL SUPERMARKET!

SALES FROM THE CRYPT

There was once a time when it was trendy to collect mummified body parts! In the 1800s and early 1900s, people in Europe loved all things Egyptian. Some would visit the country and buy mummies from sellers on the street! Those who could not afford a whole body would buy just a part, like a head or a foot. While people back then loved learning about Egypt, they did not take good care of the artifacts. Many even threw parties to unwrap the remains. Thankfully, people today have a lot more respect for history.

Catalog No. 174346

Canopic Jar

Canopic jars held organs removed during the mummification process! Each jar held a single organ and was said to be watched over by a protective god. The baboon-headed god, who is represented on this jar, was charged with protecting the lungs of the deceased!

SCARAB
BEETLE!

Catalog No. 173913

Child Sarcophagus Lid

This stone coffin, or sarcophagus, lid dates back to roughly 945 to 732 BC. The lid features a wide-eyed depiction of the deceased, a child wearing a classic headdress adorned with a scarab beetle, which is a symbol of rebirth and regeneration!

Catalog No. 166242

Egyptian Coffin Panel

Ancient Egyptians decorated their coffins with drawings of bad omens, powerful gods, and curses to scare awayl robbers! This coffin panel depicts the goddess Isis, one of the most important figures in Egyptian religion.

Walking WHALES

Whale, whale, whale... Look what we have here!

These whales aren't walking—well, at least not now! The "walking whales" are a group of ancient fossils dating back 37 million years! They were found in the shifting sands of the Egyptian Sahara, where many ancient mammals lived. The extinct creatures are relatives of the big sea animals we see today. The discovery sheds light on how whales changed from land to sea mammals. One of the fossils is a complete skeleton of a whale with legs! It measures about 65 feet (20 m) long—that's longer than a humpback whale!

WHALES ON LAND!

LONELIEST HOUSE

Say "hello" to the world's loneliest house. Located on Iceland's Ellidaey Island, it was built in the 1950s as a hunting lodge. It now stands alone on a 110-acre (44.5-hectare) island! Keeping the home company is a large population of puffins, a type of seabird. To access the house, travelers must take a boat ride across freezing, choppy waters!

ODD ONE

Twenty-five of the 26 soccer players in the Serbian national squad at the 2022 World Cup had last names ending in "ic." The odd man out was midfielder Nemanja Gudelj.

SECRET BULLET

A 95-year-old man named Zhao, from Shandong, China, discovered that he had been living with a bullet lodged in his neck for 77 years. He was likely wounded by the bullet while serving in the Chinese Army in World War II but knew nothing of the injury until he started to feel discomfort in his neck following a fall at his home in 2022. The bullet showed up on an X-ray, but doctors decided not to remove it because of the risk of intrusive surgery at Zhao's age.

FROG CITY

Frogs are everywhere in Willimantic, Connecticut. Frog Bridge has four green frog statues, the city seal shows an image of a frog, and many businesses have frog logos. It all dates back to a night in June 1754 when the sound of thousands of croaking bullfrogs in a nearby pond made people mistakenly believe they were coming under attack by either the French or Native Americans.

GRAND GENERATIONS

In 2023, 98-year-old MaeDell Taylor Hawkins from Kentucky had around 600 grandchildren spanning across six generations—including 106 grandchildren, 222 great-grandchildren, 234 great-great-grandchildren, and 37 great-great-great-grandchildren.

TATTOO ENTHUSIASTS

Zookeeper Tobias Müller and his partner Lena-Marie Duhn, from Dortmund, Germany, have a combined total of 360 tattoos and 54 body piercings. He also has a split tongue, a permanent branding, four subdermal silicone implants, and an implanted magnet and chip.

CANINE AUDIENCE

On September 11, 2022, 127 dogs attended an outdoor screening of the Disney film *101 Dalmatians* in Worcester, England.

FUKANG METEORITE

In 2000, a hiker found a rare rock in China called the Fukang meteorite! It is a pallasite, a very old rock that can teach us about the early solar system. The meteorite is almost 4.5 billion years old! The hiker sent the rock to scientists to study its colorful, stained glass appearance. It is made of both crystals and metal. The extraterrestrial rock is truly a cosmic beauty. Pieces of the meteorite can cost anywhere between $30,000 and $2 million dollars!

GLOWING TATTOOS

Based in Sydney, Australia, tattoo artist Jonny Hall uses UV-reactive ink that makes his tattoos appear black and white under ordinary light, but under ultraviolet light, they glow bright blue, yellow, and green.

SCARED TO SIT

People who suffer from the rare condition known as kathisophobia have a fear of sitting down.

PANE-FUL PROCESS

Ethiopian-born artist Natnael Mekuria, who lives in Washington, D.C., creates celebrity portraits by carefully cracking panes of special glass with a small metal chisel and a hammer. He begins by forming an outline of the image on the glass and controls the size of each crack by varying the amount of force when hitting the chisel. It took months of practice before he was able to develop a technique that stopped the glass from shattering.

NAPKIN NOTES

English composer Edward Elgar was inspired to write his Cello Concerto after surgery in London in 1918. After the operation to remove an infected tonsil, he immediately asked for a pencil and a napkin and wrote down the main theme to the concerto.

BONE BEATS

The Triceratone is a one-of-a-kind instrument made from a replica dinosaur skull! It was created for the TV show *Prehistoric Planet*. The composers needed music for a time 66 million years ago! The problem? There were no musical instruments back then. So instead, new ones were created! Also crafted for the show was a xylophone made with 200-million-year-old petrified wood and a cello made from a real moose leg bone.

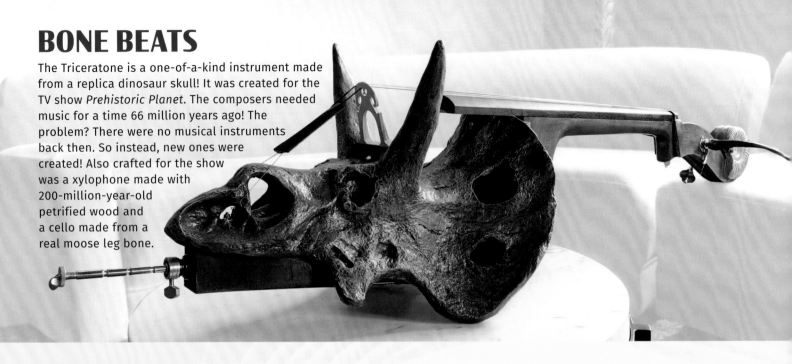

STYLISH DELIVERY
As a boy, former U.S. senator Robert Kennedy—brother of JFK—used to do a newspaper round in his family's chauffeur-driven Rolls-Royce.

MUSICAL SURGERY
A musician played the saxophone during his nine-hour brain surgery in Rome, Italy. Surgeons encouraged him to play so that they could map the different functions of his brain while they operated.

PARALLEL LIVES
Twin sisters Celci Sanner and Delci Lau, from Clarksville, Arkansas, gave birth to daughters Esme and Noelle in adjacent hospital rooms on the same day—January 31, 2023.

INFLATABLE JEANS

Swedish company Mo'cycle created airbag jeans for motorcyclists. Airbags built into the pants inflate and offer impact protection to the rider's lower body during an accident.

ARM NOSE
A woman from Toulouse, France, grew a new nose on her arm for two months. She lost a large part of her nose to cancer in 2013, forcing her to live for more than four years without a nose. Surgeons implanted a custom nose, made from 3D-printed biomaterial, onto her forearm and used a skin graft from her temple to cover it before it was transplanted onto her face.

GLUED EARS
To achieve the perfect look on her wedding day, Brazilian bride Lorena Mendes glued the backs of her ears to her head with a strong adhesive. She didn't want her ears to stick out through her hair.

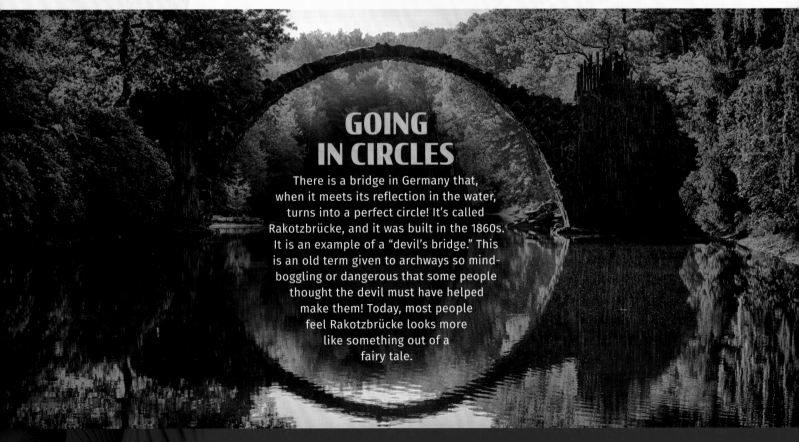

GOING IN CIRCLES

There is a bridge in Germany that, when it meets its reflection in the water, turns into a perfect circle! It's called Rakotzbrücke, and it was built in the 1860s. It is an example of a "devil's bridge." This is an old term given to archways so mind-boggling or dangerous that some people thought the devil must have helped make them! Today, most people feel Rakotzbrücke looks more like something out of a fairy tale.

LAVA-LY CATHEDRAL

The Clermont-Ferrand Cathedral in France is made of black lava rock!

The unusual material is thanks to the 80 dormant volcanoes nearby. The church's dark color and tall, delicate spires make it stand out from the rest of the city. Construction started in 1248 and took hundreds of years to finish. The inside of the church is also made from lava rock. Its black walls make the stained glass windows look even more colorful!

Curd Climb

In a game called Dahi Handi, players form a human pyramid to reach and break open pots filled with yogurt!

During the Hindu festival Krishna Janmashtami, pots of homemade yogurt, called curd, hang up to 40 feet (12 m) above game participants. That's not the only challenge, though! Onlookers throw water at the players as they try to reach the top! The game spurs from Lord Krishna's love for butter and curd, or *dahi*. Women would hang an earthen pot, or *handi*, to keep the curd out of Krishna's reach!

IT'S RAINING CURD!

HUMAN PYRAMID!

PRACTICE MAKES PERFECT

Born in the Dominican Republic, Hansel Enmanuel played as a point guard in college basketball for the Northwestern State Demons in 2022 using just one arm. He lost his left arm in an accident when he was six, but practiced for hours on court to learn how to bounce and dribble one-handed and master one-handed shots.

FESTIVAL FIGHT

Every January, the Italian coastal town of Grado stages a festival where 10 rowboats containing people dressed as sea witches land at the harbor and conduct a mock fight with local women who are armed with garlic and wooden crosses. The zombie-like witches—called the Varvuole—scream and dance as they rampage through the streets. The battle continues until they are defeated. The festival was inspired by the escapades of sixteenth-century pirates in the Adriatic Sea.

THOUSANDS OF THROWS

Washington State's Tom Steury celebrated his 82nd birthday by making his one-millionth basketball free throw. He has been practicing free throws for over 17 years, during which he has spent more than 2,500 hours on court, and estimates that he has made 94 percent of the shots.

SUCCESS FOR ALL

In a 1931 exhibition game against the New York Yankees, an 18-year-old girl named Jackie Mitchell, who was pitching for the Chattanooga Lookouts, struck out both Babe Ruth and Lou Gehrig in succession. A few days later, baseball commissioner Kenesaw Mountain Landis voided her contract, declaring that the game was too strenuous for women.

LAST CHOP

The guillotine was the official method of execution in France until the death penalty was abolished there in 1981. The last person to be guillotined in France was in 1977.

ROLLER-HOOPING

Veronica Harris, a 54-year-old from Texas, roller-skated backward while hula hooping for 33 minutes and never once allowed the hoop to touch the ground.

TUG OF CUPS

In Tsuruta, Japan, bald men play tug-of-war using suction cups on their heads! The special competition is organized by the Tsuruta City Bald Men's Club. Members of the club want to show that being bald can be cool through the sport. To play, two people are attached to suction cups by a string and sit across from each other. The person whose cup comes off first loses. People with hair can join, but those with a smooth head have a better chance at winning!

THE BRAVE AND THE BALD!

WATER LOGGED

This lake is home to an underwater ghost forest!

Kaindy Lake is found near Almaty, Kazakhstan. It was formed in 1911 when an earthquake created a natural dam in the mountains. Over time, rain filled the valley up with water. The trees poking out of the cold blue water are long dead, but there is life below the surface! Underwater, green algae cover the branches like leaves to create this eerie, yet beautiful, scene.

UNDERWATER TREES!

MEDAL REMAKE

When Germany invaded Denmark in 1940 during World War II, eminent scientists Max von Laue and James Franck stopped the Nazis from seizing their Nobel Prizes by having the 23-karat gold medals dissolved in acid by a chemist. After the war in 1950, the chemistry was reversed, and the precipitated gold was reset into medals. They were re-presented to the scientists two years later.

ACCIDENTAL JOURNEY

A 15-year-old boy who was playing hide-and-seek with friends managed to find the perfect hiding place—1,600 miles (2,560 km) away! He hid in a shipping container in his home city of Chittagong, Bangladesh, but accidentally locked himself in. He was loaded onto a ship and ended up in Malaysia six days later.

VOMITING SKILLS

A clinic in Amsterdam, the Netherlands, posted a job opening for someone who can vomit at will—and received more than 100 applicants. The successful candidate helped patients who suffer from emetophobia, a fear of vomiting.

JAIL WISH

Sixty-five-year-old Donald Santacroce held up a bank in Salt Lake City, Utah, because he wanted to be sent to federal prison. He handed a note to tellers saying that it was a robbery and asking for just $1. When asked to leave, he refused and told staff to call the police. He then sat down in the lobby and waited for the police to arrive.

FROZEN RACE

In February 2023, 75 runners took part in a half marathon race on the frozen Pangong Lake on the border of India and China, located 13,862 feet (4,226 m) above sea level with temperatures that reach –22°F (–30°C) in winter. The race lasted four hours, and all of the runners underwent six days of acclimatization before the event.

LUCKY LANE

There is a mountain trail in Kyoto, Japan, lined with thousands of bright red gates! The crimson path is part of the Fushimi Inari shrine. Founded in 711, the site is a place of worship devoted to the Shinto god of rich harvests and business success. The red gates, called *torii*, are donated by people and businesses wishing for good fortune. Because old gates get removed and new ones are often added, the exact number of torii at Fushimi Inari is always changing.

SWELL STONE

Wave Rock looks like a surfer's dream frozen in time! The granite cliff is about 50 feet (15 m) tall and roughly 360 feet (110 m) long. But don't bother bringing your board. Wave Rock is in Hyden, Western Australia—more than 100 miles (160 km) from the nearest ocean! The totally tubular shape was formed by 2.7 billion years of wind and water slow eroding the rock away.

TRUNKS, TREASURES, and TRADITIONS

elephant, Thailand's Erawan Museum is a treasure trove of art and culture.

The museum's three-headed elephant is about as tall as a nine-story building and weighs as much as 42 adult elephants! It is based on the Hindu Erawan, a divine elephant with multiple tusks and trunks. Within the museum are three levels of precious relics, art, and antiques. As soon as you enter, you're greeted by two large dragons wrapping themselves around the interior, guiding you up. Each ornate detail has been obsessively carved and painted!

DO YOU BELIEVE?

On September 12, 2023, ufologist and journalist Jamie Maussan presented what he claimed were alien bodies to the Congress of Mexico. The alleged aliens had large heads, big eyes, no teeth, and only three fingers. They were said to be found near Peru's ancient Nazca Lines and around 1,000 years old. That is, until they were reviewed by Flavio Estrada, a forensic archaeologist at the Institute of Legal Medicine of Peru. Estrada revealed the "aliens" were actually dolls made, in part, by gluing animal and human bones together.

UF... OH?

RED RIVER

The Raudarfoss waterfall in south Iceland runs red! The natural wonder's name means "waterfall in the red river" and it stands at about 66 feet (20.12 m) tall. The color comes from the iron in the Rauda River's soil. The water has different shades of red, too, like tomato juice or rusted metal!

RUSTY WATERS!

PASSENGER PUSH

The Wilmington and Long Beach Rapid Transit Railroad, which ran in the Los Angeles area in the 1880s, was operated by a steam locomotive that was so lacking in power that passengers frequently had to climb out of the coaches and push the train up the steeper sections of the track.

UNICORN HUNT

Michigan's Lake Superior State University has been issuing unicorn hunting licenses since 1971, after one of the university's directors wanted to add a little magic (and press attention) to the campus. Hunting is encouraged all year round, except for Valentine's Day and Christmas.

MUMMY FRIEND

Julio Cesar Bermejo of Puno, Peru, carried a mummified human corpse in a cooler bag. He revealed that the remains, estimated to be between 600-800 years old, were his friend and they shared a room. His father brought home the mummified body 30 years earlier when he couldn't donate it to a museum.

MAYO ROMANCE

On November 19, 2022, 72-year-old Brenda Williams and 78-year-old Dennis Delgado were married in aisle eight of Fry's grocery store in Casa Grande, Arizona, where they had first met a year earlier while searching for mayonnaise.

NOODLE NOTES

Nittanosho Kanzantei, a restaurant in Ota, Japan, sells noodles with religious calligraphy printed on them. The Buddhist scriptures, which are edible, remain visible even after cooking, so customers can read their food while eating it.

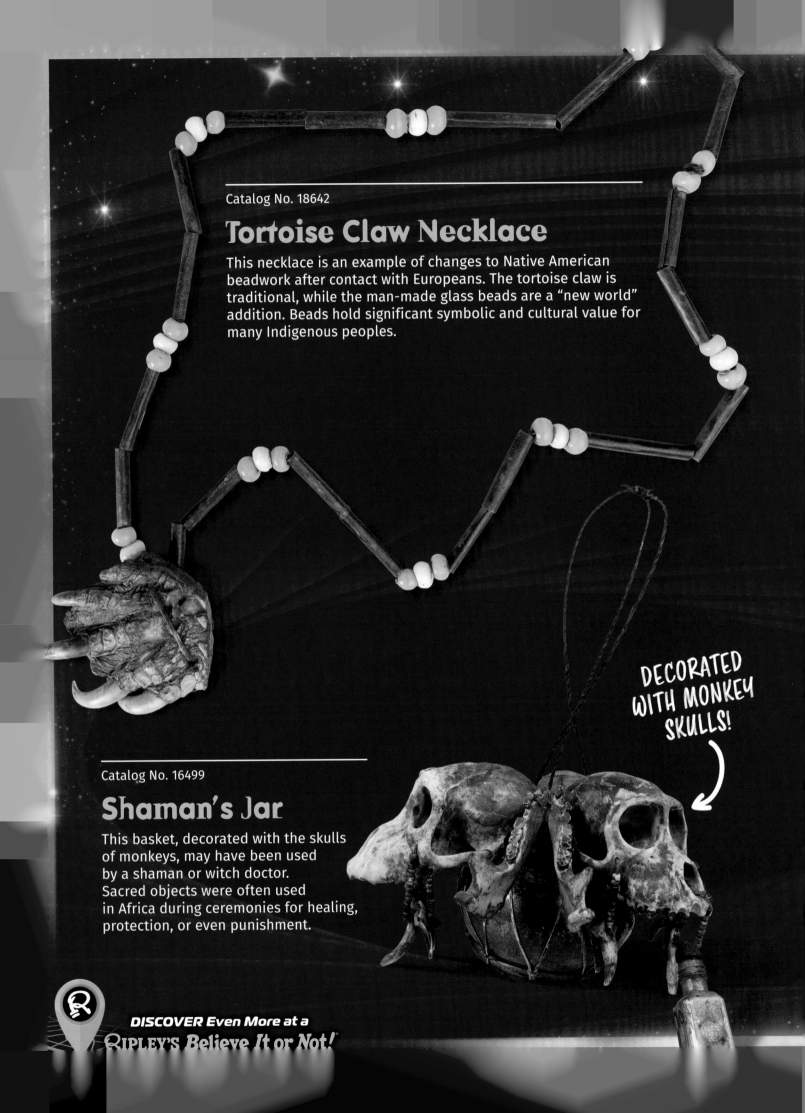

Catalog No. 18642

Tortoise Claw Necklace

This necklace is an example of changes to Native American beadwork after contact with Europeans. The tortoise claw is traditional, while the man-made glass beads are a "new world" addition. Beads hold significant symbolic and cultural value for many Indigenous peoples.

Catalog No. 16499

Shaman's Jar

This basket, decorated with the skulls of monkeys, may have been used by a shaman or witch doctor. Sacred objects were often used in Africa during ceremonies for healing, protection, or even punishment.

DECORATED WITH MONKEY SKULLS!

DISCOVER *Even More at a*
RIPLEY'S *Believe It or Not!*

Catalog No. 11289

Guro Dance Mask

The Guro people of the Ivory Coast don unique masks during their cultural dance known as Zaouli. Each mask can take up to six days to make and is crafted from hand-carved wood. The mask is worn by a designated Zaouli dancer, who is believed to then be possessed and moved by the spirit of the mask.

Catalog No. 16416

Temple Bull

Nandi, meaning "happiness" or "joy," is the bull of the Hindu god Shiva. This figure symbolizes qualities like purity, and justice.

PLANET *Jellies*

Dive deep into the otherworldly lives of jellies! From a species the size of a grape to one that lives upside down, jellies put even the most bizarre science fiction creatures to shame.

I'M PICKIN' UP DINNER TONIGHT!

MANGROVE BOX JELLY

One of the smallest jellies in the ocean, the mangrove box jelly is only about the size of a grape! But what makes it really special is its shape. Instead of being round, the bell of the mangrove box jelly is cube-shaped! Despite its small size and odd figure, it is a fast swimmer and can reach speeds of up to 4.6 mph (7.4 kmph)!

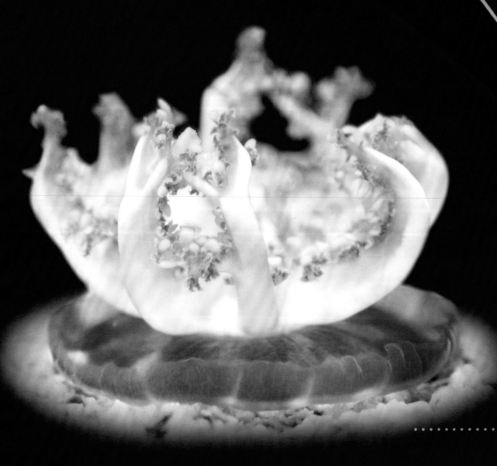

UPSIDE-DOWN JELLY

It's a topsy-turvy world for the upside-down jelly. It lives in shallow waters near mangroves, with its bell on the bottom and its arms reaching up! This is to help get sunlight to algae living in its arms. In return for giving them a sunny place to live, the algae provide the jelly with almost all of its food!

ATOLLA JELLY

The atolla jelly lives so deep in the ocean that its vibrant red body looks black! This helps it hide from danger, but sometimes a predator can still find it. When this happens, the atolla jelly confuses the hungry hunter by flashing bright blue lights from its body! This is why it is also known as the alarm jelly.

CAULIFLOWER JELLY

Does this creature remind you of a certain vegetable? The cauliflower jelly lives in the open waters of the Indo-Pacific and Atlantic Ocean. It is eaten as a delicacy in China and Japan, making its food-inspired name even more fitting!

WHITE-SPOTTED JELLY

If this jelly had social media, it would be a travel blogger! Although native to the Southwest Pacific, this species is all over the world today. How? By hitching rides on ships! But the white-spotted jelly is an unwelcome tourist. It eats more than its fair share and makes life harder for local animals.

PLASTIC PYRAMID

A new pyramid appeared in Egypt in late 2022—but this one was made from 20 tons of plastic!

It was built to mark the start of the 100YR CLEANUP project led by Zero Co and The Hidden Sea. To make the pyramid, the groups teamed up with locals to remove trash from the Nile River. They collected more than one million water bottles' worth of plastic! The end result was a pyramid taller than a three-story building. It showed how serious our plastic waste problem is. But there is hope. Cleanup projects like this one and using less plastic are just the start!

ZANY HOTEL

A short ride from Amsterdam in the Netherlands, you'll find Zaandam, home to the Inntel Hotel. From the outside, it looks like an 11-story stack of regional cottages (almost 70 of them!). However, one blue cottage stands out. It is a reference to Monet's painting, *The Blue House*, completed in Zaandam in 1871. Architect Wilfried van Winden's inspiration came from the idea that the hotel is your temporary cottage home.

CANDLE-THON!

There is something very colorful at the Inka Grill restaurant in Cusco, Peru. It's not a painting or a decoration, but a huge pile of wax! This is no ordinary pile of wax, though. It has grown from more than 20 years of burning candles in the restaurant. Over decades of birthdays, meals, and celebrations, the candles were lit and their wax dripped down to create this unusual, colorful mountain, adding a little magic to each meal!

FAMILY GRADUATION

Over the course of nearly 70 years, 44 members of the Wuensche family have graduated from Texas Tech University in Lubbock, Texas. The first, Francis Wuensche Holden, graduated in 1953 and four generations later, Andrew Simnacher graduated in 2021.

DIFFERENT DAYS

When Argentine soccer player Gonzalo Higuain scored twice for Inter Miami in a game against Columbus Crew in 2022, his goals were netted on different days. The game started at 8 p.m. on September 13 and Higuain scored his first goal at 8:25 p.m., but play was then delayed by a lightning storm. The game restarted at 11:35 p.m., with Higuain scoring his second goal—an 82nd-minute winner—at 12:13 a.m. on September 14.

BIRTHDAY GUY

Dennis Garsjo has memorized the birthdays of nearly 3,000 residents in Glasgow, Montana, (population 3,202) so that he can greet them on the street. "The Birthday Guy," as he is known, says he inherited the talent from his mother who knew the birthdays of 126 relatives.

QUICK TRIP

It took three people just 5 days 13 hours 10 minutes to visit all 50 U.S. states. Peter McConville and Pavel Krechetov, from Austin, Texas, teamed up with Abdullahi Salah, from Minneapolis, Minnesota. They started in Vermont and traveled by car through 48 states to Washington State before flying to Alaska and Hawaii, covering a total distance of over 7,200 miles (11,520 km).

CAT COLLECTIBLES

Shawn Redner and his wife, Hilary, have a collection of more than 13,000 cat figurines and cat-themed pieces of art. They display a selection in the basement of their home in Menomonee Falls, Wisconsin, a house also known as Redner's Rescued Cat Figurine Mewseum.

CRAB-ULOUS CREATIONS

The sand bubbler crab covers beaches in patterns made from hundreds of tiny little balls of sand! The small crab comes out of its burrow to look for food when the tide is low. To feed, it puts sand in its mouth and eats the tiny animals living inside. Then it spits the sand out in the form of a ball! The sand bubbler is small, but it works fast. The 0.4-inch-wide (1-cm) crab can search through all the sand within 3.3 feet (1 m) of its home in just a couple hours!

SPIT IT OUT!

BRAIN BOOST

To boost reproduction following the death of their queen, female worker Indian jumping ants can shrink and regrow their brains.

CRAB CARE

A parasitic barnacle, *Sacculina carcini*, not only attaches itself to crabs, but it also turns male crabs into females so they can care for the barnacle's eggs.

BIRTHDAY BALLOONS

The balloons that Kason Johnson was given at his school in Mountain Grove, Missouri, to mark his eighth birthday seemed lost forever when they floated away—but they were found a few days later 500 miles (800 km) away in Cleveland, Tennessee. And Todd Huyler, the man who found them, gave Kason $100 as a birthday gift.

SCORPION TRAINING

Meerkat parents carefully train their offspring in the art of hunting scorpions. Adult meerkats bite the stinger off a live scorpion and give it to their young so that they can practice killing and eating it without getting stung.

TINY TERRIER

In the 1940s, Arthur Marples, from Blackburn, England, owned a dwarf Yorkshire terrier dog that was only 2.8 inches (7 cm) tall and measured just 3.75 inches (9.4 cm) from nose to tail, making the tiny dog about the size of a human fist.

SNAKE SURVIVAL

Sharon Hughes' pet cat Jaffa has survived being bitten three times by venomous snakes near their home in Horsham, Australia.

POOP BOMB

When threatened by another bird, the fieldfare—a member of the thrush family—will force the bird to the ground, fly up, and deliberately poop on it. The poop bomb can be fatal because if the feces sticks to the grounded bird's wings, it will be unable to fly.

SKY SPIRAL

People watching Alaska's northern lights on April 15, 2023, were in for a shock when a wormhole seemed to appear in the sky!

The strange blue spiral was not made by aliens, but it did come from a rocket on its way to space! Earlier that night, the SpaceX Falcon 9 rocket launched from California. It released its unused fuel a few hours later as it flew over Alaska. The water vapor in the exhaust turned into ice in the sky. The blue spiral was light bouncing off the ice! The rare sight lasted about seven minutes. The photographer who took this picture, Todd Salat, called it "one of the most bizarre experiences" of his life.

Wings *that* WOW!

The Picasso moth (*Baorisa hieroglyphica*) has wings that look like Pablo Picasso paintings!

The moth has a 2-inch (5-cm) wingspan with lines and shapes that look like they were painted on. The special insect has been called "the most interesting moth in the world" and is found in Asia and India. The insect is also great at hiding because its colorful wings help it blend in with the plants around it. The Picasso moth is both a work of art and a thing of nature!

NATURE'S MASTERPIECE!

POTATO DOG

Chris Gittins, a former school principal, found a dog-shaped potato in his harvest! The spud has what looks like the legs, tail, and head of a bully dog. Chris refuses to eat this potato! He often finds oddly shaped vegetables where he lives in Berkshire, England. Chris says this is the weirdest one he's found.

MAN'S BEST POTATO?

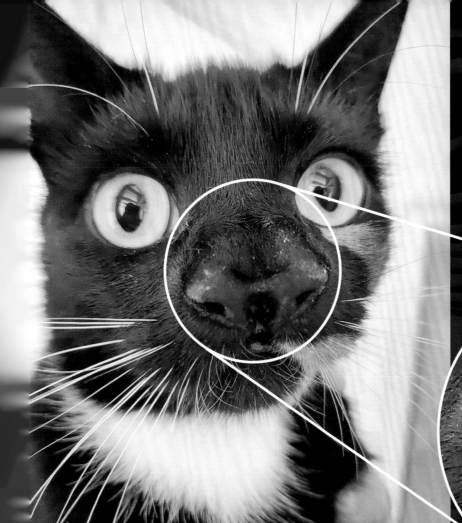

TWO-NOSED CAT

Nanny McPhee may look like she has a large nose, but it is actually two! A vet check revealed that this unique cat has a rare congenital abnormality. Despite her extra nose, Nanny McPhee is totally healthy! Nanny was given to the Cats Protection Adoption Centre in Warrington, England, where she was swiftly adopted. In fact, Nanny was the 590th cat at the rescue to find their forever home in 2023!

OFFICER HOP

In 2023, Yuba City Police Department in California appointed a rescue rabbit named Percy as its wellness officer. The lost rabbit was found in the middle of Percy Avenue and was adopted by a police services analyst before being promoted to the rank of Officer Percy to act as a support animal.

MIGRATION MARVEL

In October 2022, a five-month-old bar-tailed godwit flew—without stopping—8,425 miles (13,560 km) in 11 days, from Alaska to the Australian state of Tasmania, for its winter migration.

SPEEDY PEELER

Pang Pha, an Asian elephant at Zoo Berlin in Germany, has taught herself to peel bananas with her trunk—and she can do it faster than a human. Researchers believe she may have watched humans peeling bananas for her and is imitating them.

ONE-WAY WALK

Ducklings follow their mothers in single-file formation to conserve energy in the same way that runners, cyclists, and race cars draft behind each other in a race.

RAVEN WATCH

A group of ravens permanently guard the Tower of London—but they can be dismissed for bad behavior. According to legend, at least six ravens must always be in residence at the Tower to prevent the collapse of the British monarchy. In 1986, one bird, George, who had served for 11 years, was fired after he had destroyed five TV antennas in a week. More recently, Bran was discharged because he was too aggressive toward humans.

GOAT BUSTERS

In September 2022, a male goat was arrested after damaging property and chasing a person around a car in Tonopah, Arizona. When cornered by police, the goat urinated on the sheriff's deputy.

DEEP DIVER

A species of snailfish was filmed swimming in the Izu-Ogasawara Trench, south of Japan, more than 5 miles (8 km) below the water surface.

SUPER SHARP

The North American porcupine has about 30,000 quills, and each quill has up to 800 barbs near the tip to help penetrate flesh.

BOLTING BEETLE

The Australian tiger beetle can run at a speed of 171 body lengths per second. That would be like an adult human running at 720 mph (1,159 kmph)—almost as fast as the speed of sound.

FIRST FLIGHT

The first passenger airplane service from the UK to Australia began in 1935 from London to Brisbane and took 12.5 days!

WALL PAPER

The walls, doors, and even furniture of the Rockport Paper House in Rockport, Massachusetts, are made completely of varnished newspapers!

Roughly 100,000 newspapers were used to create this house in 1922. Builder Elis F. Stenman went to great lengths to make this marvel last. Each wall panel is made of 215 layers of paper stuck together with homemade glue made from flour, water, and apples. The result is surprisingly sturdy! Each piece of front-page furniture is functional, too—even the clock, which features newspapers from 48 U.S. states!

215 LAYERS OF PAPER!

CALL THE INFANTRY!

CREEPY CRAWLERS

The Žižkov Television Tower in Prague, Czech Republic, is home to the *Miminka*—10 huge baby sculptures that each weigh 772 pounds (350 kg)! Created by artist David Černý, each of the babies is about 11.5 feet (3.5 m) long and 8.5 feet (2.6 m) tall. They were first added to the tower in 2000 as temporary art installations. People went so goo-goo gaga over them that the sculptures were made permanent.

SO ROMANTIC!

WINGS OF LOVE

Behind the bright butterflies on this home is a beautiful love story! Once upon a time, J and Sonja Jackson moved to a small house in Pacific Grove, California. Soon, Sonja began having trouble seeing. One day, J painted her a beautiful wooden butterfly. She could see its bright colors! As a labor of love, J covered their home in hundreds more of the paintings. The couple no longer lives there, but the house still delights visitors and hopeless romantics alike!

LIVING WALLS

Artists used real plants to turn a plain, boring wall into a living work of art! The mural blends nature with people's faces in fun ways. Long tufts of grass take the place of a man's bushy mustache. A woman's curly hair is actually thousands of green leaves! Located in London, the playful painting was made with the help of a local youth club. The living wall celebrates the area's history and culture. It also shows how art and nature can work together to make the world a better place.

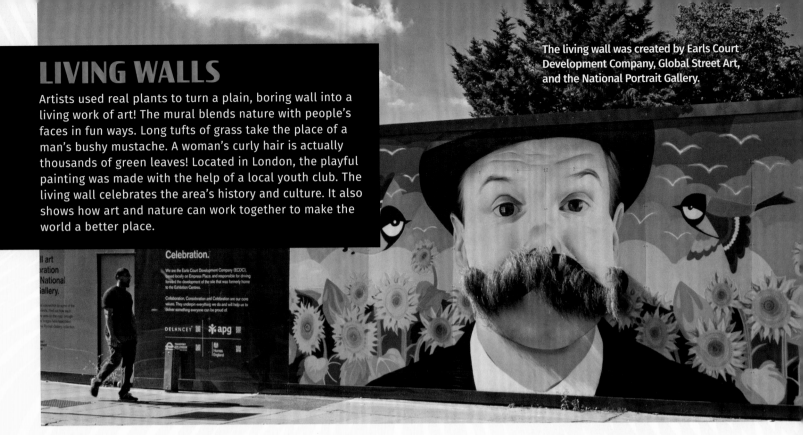

The living wall was created by Earls Court Development Company, Global Street Art, and the National Portrait Gallery.

TOILET RING

After 21 years, Nick and Shaina Day, from Lakeland, Florida, were reunited with Shaina's diamond engagement ring. It had been accidentally flushed down the toilet at Nick's parents' home two decades earlier. They had searched for it at the time, but they eventually gave up and purchased a replacement. Then, in 2022, a plumber found the ring lodged inside the toilet bowl!

TOMB CURSE?

In 1973, within weeks of opening a tomb that was thought to be cursed, 10 scientists died suddenly. The tomb belonged to King Casimir IV of Poland and his wife, Elizabeth of Austria, and had been undisturbed for nearly 500 years. It later emerged that there was a more likely explanation for the deaths—in opening the tomb, the scientists had inhaled a deadly fungus, later found inside.

LONG-LOST PHOTOS

When a fisherman saved a camera and its photos from the riverbed of Colorado's Animas, little did he know it had been there for 13 years. Spencer Greiner posted the pictures to a local Facebook group and found its owner, Coral Amayi, who recalled the loss in 2010.

HOLE IN HISTORY

In 1829, the greenkeeper at Musselburgh Golf Club in Scotland is said to have used a 4.25-inch-wide (10.6-cm) piece of drainage pipe to cut a hole in the green. That measurement was later adopted by the game's governing body, and today golf holes all over the world measure the exact same diameter, just because it happened to be the width of drainage pipes in Musselburgh 200 years ago.

WRONG SCOTT

An invite to compete at the 2023 Masters golf tournament was sent to the wrong Scott Stallings. It was accidentally sent to an occasional golfer in Georgia named Scott Stallings instead of to the Tennessee-based pro golfer of the same name, who was ranked number 54 in the world at the time. Coincidentally, both men have wives named Jennifer.

HOLD THE PHONE!

For more than 30 years, hundreds of Garfield-shaped phones have washed up on the beaches of northwestern France! They first appeared in the 1980s and have kept showing up ever since. In 2018, more than 200 Garfield phone pieces littered the beaches! The source of the lasagna-loving feline phones was a mystery until recently. In 2019, a tip from local farmer René Morvan broke the case wide open. Decades ago, he and his brother were exploring deep within a seaside cave during low tide and found a shipping container. It was filled with Garfield phones!

TROPICAL TWISTS AND TURNS

The Pineapple Garden Maze in Oahu, Hawaii, stretches across more than 3 acres (1.2 hectares) and has more than 14,000 plants!

Made by the Dole Plantation in 1998, the maze has almost 2.5 miles (4 km) of curvy paths to explore. And the fun doesn't stop there! Hidden in the maze are stations with fun facts about Hawaii's eight biggest islands. The goal is to find all eight stations and make your way out as fast as you can! Most people take about 40 minutes to finish the maze, but some have done it in less than 8 minutes! Think you can beat that?

Catalog No. 169961

Stamp Art

Created by Peter Mason of Gloucestershire, England, this portrait of the Statue of Liberty is created entirely from hundreds of postage stamps! The stamps are of three denominations: two-cent Frank Lloyd Wright issues, 13-cent Liberty Bells, and 32-cent Statue of Liberties.

Catalog No. 175656

Banksy Bucks

Banksy, the elusive, anonymous artist, printed £1,000,000 worth of fake currency that he titled *Di-faced Tenners* in 2004. The artist released some of these works by dropping a briefcase full of the counterfeit bills at the Liverpool Street tube station during rush hour!

Catalog No. 1625

Continuous Line Drawing

This frequently painted founding father has never been seen like this before! This one-line portrait of George Washington was drawn entirely without lifting the pen from the page.

Glass Act

Eriko Kobayashi's glass sculptures look good enough to eat!

Eriko fell in love with glass making in 2014. She has since studied the art in both her native Japan and the U.S., where she now lives in Seattle. Eriko uses special methods and materials for her work. One of them is a glass clay that she can shape without intense heat. Some of the glassy foods she has made include pizza, s'mores, crackers, and gummy bears! With her realistic sculptures, Eriko invites viewers to take a closer look and think more deeply about them.

THIS IS NOT REAL FOOD!

MAKING GLASS NOODLES!

Index

Numbers

DISCOVER a World WHERE...

Your Ripley's adventure—through the pages of this book—has only just begun! Explore unique wonders, enter an underwater realm, and embark on your next adventure at Ripley's—where unbelievable experiences become unforgettable family memories. It's time to let curiosity be your guide!

WHERE NATURE BECOMES YOUR PLAYGROUND!

WHERE SUPERHEROES ARE WAITING TO MEET YOU!

WHERE THINGS AREN'T QUITE AS THEY SEEM!